LEAVERS
TO LEADERS

LEAVERS
TO LEADERS

7 Steps to Reinvent Yourself
While in Transition

SAMUEL T. REDDY

Book production by Oxford Literary Consultancy.

www.oxfordwriters.com

Foreword

Paul Bennett – Director of Enterprise, Southampton Business School, University of Southampton

There can be little doubt we are now living in a time of unprecedented change. The fourth industrial revolution has given rise to globalisation, and the unrelenting acceleration of technological advances has created a business landscape that is ever more complex, globally connected and competitive. Success in this new world order may require a different leadership response.

How can leaders best prepare to thrive and succeed in the new world order?

How will leaders ensure their organisations are fit for the future? In the coming years, businesses will not only be measured by what they do, but also by how they do it, and how value is created.

More than ever before, leaders will need to be the instigators of innovation and enable their talented people to thrive in uncertain environments. It is unlikely in the future, that any one individual leader will be able to fully understand and deal with the high density of complex challenges facing them, alone. This suggests future leadership success could be dependent upon more collaborative and adaptive leadership approaches.

During uncertainty, employees, clients and shareholders migrate to the people and organisations they trust. What will leaders need to do, to maintain trust? How will they develop a leadership agenda that is intelligent and purposeful in the face of social, technological, environmental, economic, political, legal and ethical scrutiny?

The character and integrity of the individual leader will matter, as will their ability to lead themselves, lead others and lead within their organisation in any given context. These three elements are critical and will require rigorous continuous development if a leader is to remain relevant and capable of leading successfully into the future.

I believe the Leaders Operating System contained in this book provides a very accessible and rigorous approach to leader development. It also provides a call to arms, to do what needs to be done, to be a fit for future leader.

I have known Samuel for a little over three years and he is without doubt one of the most tenacious, capable, and likeable individuals I have ever met. Samuel is a true thought leader and has the enviable ability of translating his thoughts into practical and actionable processes. In this authoritative book, he provides an integrated system of development tools which can be used by all leaders at all levels within an organisation.

Paul Bennett is Director of Enterprise, Southampton Business School, University of Southampton. He is an elected member of the Board of Trustees of the Chartered Management Institute. He is an authority on leadership and management development, a professional speaker and a trusted adviser to Board members and Senior Leadership Teams in industry.

GENERAL SIR RICHARD BARRONS KCB CBE

Thousands of sailors, marines, soldiers, airmen and airwomen leave their Service every year around the world. Whether they served their country in uniform for a few years or several decades, they all have in common that they took up arms, joining a vocation that required them to be committed, resilient, expert, and fit. They lived lives with very little separation between life and work, where everybody relies on each other – prepared if necessary to lay down their life for the man or woman next to them in the fight, as well as for their family, unit and country.

We all have to leave our Service at some time. Some leave as a result of itchy feet, some due to the toll of the tough exigencies of military life, a few through injury or illness, and many just because they got older. With very few exceptions, everybody of every rank and Service finds it hard when they leave. Of course, there are some immediate advantages: on finally taking off uniform there is more personal freedom to go where you want to and do what you please, the opportunity to try new things, free of the obligations that come with military service. But almost every leaver soon finds they have parted with a vocation, a way of life, that gave them purpose and self-respect, that felt like it really mattered, that developed them as individuals and found them lifelong friends. This is true, paradoxically, even for many of those who leave unhappy and determined to get out.

The step back into civilian life reveals a very different way of living and working. It's not that it is necessarily bad, but it is necessarily very different. The prospects are actually good, many civilians seem to thrive in contented lives flush with more money than anybody in uniform will ever earn. If they want to, civilians can seize all the benefits of life that prosperous, liberal and safe societies can offer. On the other hand, there is no obvious vocation to commit to unless there is another aspect of public service to join, no longer the excitement of operations or the sense of belonging that military service engenders. The point is, the transition feels hard, because it is hard. Perhaps the greatest tragedy around military service is not the friends who never returned from battle, or the life-changing mental and physical injuries some of us must bear, it is the thousands and thousands of veterans who find themselves apparently trapped in jobs that employ a fraction of their character, skill and experience, miserable through working for muppets for pennies, when with a little help they could be setting the world alight with their energy, entrepreneurial spirit, and leadership.

This is where 'Leavers to Leaders' makes a difference. Based on Sammy Reddy's personal experience, not always a smooth ride by any means, and his energetic devotion to his own self-improvement and to helping those who also served, he offers a guide to us all on how to make that transition work. The seven action steps have been forged by contact with the hard-nosed, transactional, and charlatan-infested realities of commercial life. The book offers positive advice about what to expect and how to deal with it. I commend it to everybody who is making their transition run and knows they need a compass and a map. Sammy's own journey shows what can be done, I hope everybody who reads it goes on to show what they can do too.

Dedication

I dedicate this book to my mother – your love and
guidance have made me all that I am.

To my family: my wife, my sister and my three daughters,
thank you for your support and love.

And finally to the wider Military family past and present.

Book Endorsements

"*A thoughtfully written book, which is also thought provoking and challenges the reader. Samuel brings to life his wealth of knowledge and experience to inspire, and highlights the lessons to be learnt. The book is a must-read for business leaders managing, adapting to and keeping pace with change.*"

– Sandeep Sesodia, Chairman of the Southampton Business Strategy Group, Hampshire Chamber of Commerce and a non-executive Director of the Hampshire Chamber of Commerce.

"*Applying his learning and training from years in the military, Samuel's thought-provoking book shows why and how we need to reinvent ourselves in a new digital age. It's quite possible for those in their twenties to scale up to global presence in less than a decade. It's increasingly likely that workers will have leaders younger than them. Power in the workplace could be in the hands of 30 year olds, not those in their fifties and sixties, and this might be the first era in which experience could be viewed as a liability rather than an asset. Therefore it's essential that to stay current and valuable, we may all need to re-evaluate who (and how) we are – and repeat this as required. Samuel's concepts are a wake-up call and he shows the methods, using the LOS concept, by which we can learn the lessons to be inspired, be genuine and be relevant today.*"

– Jane Malyon, author of
Scone or Scon(e) – The Essential Guide to British Afternoon Tea.

"*It's a real pleasure to be asked by Samuel to write an endorsement for this amazing book. Occasionally in life, you come across truly inspirational people. Samuel is one of those people. Not only is he a true success in his own right, but he is also one of those wonderful human beings who is prepared to share his insights into how that success came about.*

In this book you will find the 'success' formula that eludes so many people."

– Steve Jones, Author of
Turning on your P.R.O.F.I.T.S Tap. International Speaker on
employee engagement and Leadership Specialist.

"If you are only going to buy one book to help you take your career to the next level, make it this one! Comprehensive, inspiring, full of insightful exercises, and up-to-date information on how to become a leader in your industry."

– Errol Lawson, author of
The 5 Core Abilities of Highly Effective Leaders, Entrepreneur, Coach
and Motivational Speaker at Emerge Leadership UK.

"Samuel Reddy's book provides a really useful roadmap for ambitious servicemen and women who are exploring and setting out on the exciting entrepreneurial journey by setting up their own business. Working with so many micro and small businesses in the New Forest, I know just how valuable it is to nurture and support businesspeople in the earliest days of their journey from employee to employer, from following orders to placing orders, from spending other people's money to investing their own money! It is a challenging journey, but a very rewarding one, which will be helped in so many ways by Samuel's clear and encouraging advice."

– Matthew Lawson, Chairman of
the New Forest Business Partnership.

"Without a doubt, a must-read if you are embarking on a new career or leaving the forces. An incredible, holistic approach for guiding you forward in your career choice. This book will help you discover your inner leader: you will learn not only lead yourself but those around you, filling your life with opportunity, happiness, and conviction, ultimately living a life of meaning."

– Sebastian Bates, Best-Selling Author and Founder of
The Warrior Academy, a Global Martial Arts Organisation.

"As a recently retired civil servant, I find this book very informative and inspiring. The author adopts a pragmatic approach to help people find the way forward in their career choice. There are lots of useful and thoughtful ideas and actions to surface and shape the things that matter when looking for direction upon retirement or leaving the Services."

– Kin Kwong Cheung, retired
Chief Superintendent from Hong Kong Police.

"Mark Twain once said that the secret of a successful book is to: write what you know. I have read few authors in recent years who have demonstrated that as plainly as Samuel Reddy. As a master in the skill of clear communication, he brings his knowledge to the task of guiding people who have that innate desire to do hard things well, which is the cornerstone of challenging the world, and making a success of it.

What is the secret of this book's achievement? The author served between 2001 and 2006 in the Armed Forces, developing his skill sets in logistical management which travelled across Army, Navy and Air Force, in a remarkable progression from the Royal Fusiliers, a front-line infantry regiment, to the Royal Logistical Corps. His foundation gives power to the task of self-invention, or reinvention, and leads the reader to making that task both feasible and worthwhile.

I foresee that many people will be guided by this book to achieve their own success in life."

– Dr Simon Daniels, PhD, Solicitor,
Course Leader, Solent University

"A practical and well-written book full of exercises and advice. Equally useful if you are feeling 'stuck' in your current role and looking to climb up the ladder or if you want to move into something completely different."

– Jacqui Mann, Author of
Recruit, Inspire & Retain. Founder of J Mann Associates.

Contents

Leavers to Leaders

Introduction

You are reading this book because you want a change in your life that is solid and lasting. You've already achieved a certain level of success in your workplace, but still you feel that you were made for greater things. However, with this desire for change comes challenges and obstacles. The question you are facing now is a new one. How can you elevate yourself to the position you desire?

What if I told you that by reading this book and applying its core principles, you could remove all of your transition-related frustrations and fears? That you could be a great leader at all levels who shares a vision, has a passion and is accountable.

Believe it or not, you already have everything you need to make the change as a leaver to a leader. At the core of the 7 steps you will find the 3 LOS (Leader's Operating System) that will enable you to accomplish all of the above, just as those I interviewed have been doing for years.

Through life experience, I have developed a practical but thorough method to help strengthen you from a leaver to a leader.

The world has changed, in the last ten years we have seen a shift in the work place. We see checkouts at the shops being automated, we have cars ready to be driverless, we have cashiers being replaced by machines, we have TV on demand and online accounting software. Five years ago the world was in a different place. The digital transformation is shaping our way of lives from banking to retail, to entertainment, to food services. Virtually every company in every industry is shifting how they engage with customers and the markets. Perhaps the three major disruptors that we can all relate to would be Uber, Airbnb and Deliveroo. Then, along came Google Chrome, and several incredible products and services have been invented. A major player in the computer world is the iPad which was launched in January 2010 – just eight years ago! Airbnb was founded in 2007 and took off after the 2008 recession for people to easily find and book inexpensive places to stay. The music industry was revolutionised by Spotify which was launched in 2008 in Stockholm, Sweden. Oculus VR started in June 2012 in California. Now, we have the Oculus Go headset. If you are an Instagram fan, Instagram itself was launched in October 2010, with now a billion users. GPS on smartphones became commercialised in 2008/2009 (although it has been used by the military since 1978). The digital age brings quick and continual change. When you think about it, no transition that has occurred in the history has been driven by human wishes.

Change did not happen because people suddenly got fed up with their way of life and wanted a different one, simply because they found it amusing to do so.

It took one thousand years for the Agricultural Revolution to come to the surface. The change from an agricultural society to an industrial society based on manufacturing and chemical power was much faster. The digital age is driven by artificial intelligence and therefore it is likely to be happening more rapidly. It is just at its infancy and if you fail to perceive the great changes happening around us, it is because you do not desire to see that the future of a leader beyond 2020 is at risk if you are not prepared properly.

In this book, we look at the far-reaching impact of the digital revolution and help you to look at the jobs which are at risk in the next 5-10 years. We can already see the collapse of the welfare state or NHS and the capacity for gig employers to supply regular jobs on demand. The typical work is now disrupted everywhere and even the military is using technology to reduce human casualties caused by sending troops on the ground.

The military is the foremost organisation created to enable you to reinvent yourself from the day you are enlisted and frame yourself in such a way where settling down is a matter of a few weeks or months. Right from the outset, you are part of a system which is continuously changing. From your basic training, you are in the reinvention mode to change your thinking from a civilian to a military mindset. Prior to joining your basic training, you go through a selection process and decide where you best fit and find your future trade. Basic training makes you a military person, helps find your strengths and team ability, and gets you ready to face the front line. Advanced training is more about perfecting your skills and focusing on being what is called a "functional" person. Some of these skills can take a long time to develop, but by the end of it you will be a fully trained soldier while also being very functional. You then become part of a team, an organisation where everyone has been through the same process as you, but still in the same shift system as they continue to develop themselves to the highest level. In the end you have become a military person with a functional role ready for front line action, also ready to do your day-to-day job.

The economic responsibility is shifting into the hands of leaders who are completely responsible for their own destiny. The leaders will become entrepreneurial – like a private consultant, a private contractor – and in complete control of his or her finances.

The 3 LOS explores all the social and financial consequences of this rapid digital revolution and helps leaders to take advantage of the opportunity of this new age by reinventing themselves and avoiding being destroyed by the impact.

During this process, should you be fully committed to reinventing yourself into a different role, then the option is open and a system is in place to allow this transition. By the time you have completed your service, you are once again placed into a system to reinvent yourself in the civilian world. For the baby boomers, taking the shift has more or less been easy as they resettle into a civilian world. After all, they are the generation who have been pushing the economy from day one. However, for the echo boomers, also known as Generation X (those born from 1965 to 1979 and who joined the work force in the late 90s and who are now in their 40s) the experience is not going to be the same. We are now in a digital age of the (IOT) Internet of Things [1] and the future beyond 2020 has already changed. However, I have no doubt that the military personnel are the ones who will strive and become the leaders, should they realise the mountain of value that they already are standing on, and become the leaders they are trained to be. This is possible due to their ongoing development and shift mindset and anyone can learn those skills. However, it is becoming more and more challenging to do so, even for the military personnel. Those who get complacent and fail to develop and align for the future will struggle.

While I was in active service in the British Armed Forces, I reinvented myself twice like many of my peers who perhaps had the opportunity to reskill themselves, but I carried on using the same system to continuously reinvent myself now in my business life. So, if you are a business leader and reading this book, your industry is also changing every two years. Inside the 7 steps, I have highlighted the key points learned from the

[1] https://en.wikipedia.org/wiki/Internet_of_things The **Internet of Things** (**IoT**) is the network of devices, vehicles, and home appliances that contain electronics, software, actuators, and connectivity which allows these things to connect, interact and exchange data.

military that can further your business life by adapting to change and reinventing your business.

These digital platforms are mostly global and until we have a global regulation, no national or local government is able to control them. The way you interact with your clients and generate leads has also changed. But, most importantly, once you realise the change and take steps to reinvent yourself, your business will change with you.

Earlier, I mentioned the unrivalled skills we get from the military. Front line soldiers have a day-to-day functional role, but I have discovered that this system is also applicable to anyone in the civilian world who is looking to become a leader in the digital age. In order to succeed, you need to have unrivalled skills: skills to listen, learn, liven up others, lead opportunity, lead yourself, lead others and finally lead an organisation.

As I write this book, I am in the process of reinventing myself and my business for the fifth time. I was once told by an OC (Officer in Command), "You are smart but you still have a very strong French accent and to be an officer, you need to work on that." I did just that but also went further by becoming a linguist for the British Armed Forces liaising with the French military. Perhaps he didn't see the value that he contributed to my success. LOS is a timeless, practical, universal set of principles that have been in use by people from very different parts of the world. I have been through the LOS system from the early age of 22. This is not management theory, LOS is working every day.

The seven key components to reinvent yourself go right to the roots of the most important aspects of your life, the Leader's Operating System (LOS), and strengthen them. LOS is a method – even a way of life – that will help you crystallise your vision and achieve what you want.

I will cover the importance of the acronym, S.E.R.V.E in Chapter 7 and how it is by only putting others first, whether it is work colleagues or your organisation, you can better lead them.

It is quite normal to worry and be uncomfortable, but I am constantly reminded of "the importance of getting comfortable being uncomfortable" as you will find out with my personal experiences in both the British military and as an entrepreneur in business.

The principles and methods outlined in the 3 LOS (Leader's Operating System) have been designed to help anyone military and specially non-military who are looking to reinvent themselves using the military way. We will look at some of the reports and industries where employment automation is at high risk, medium and low risk and how they will undoubtedly affect you as a leader.

CHAPTER 1

Leavers to Leaders Lead Opportunity

Opportunity is Nowhere

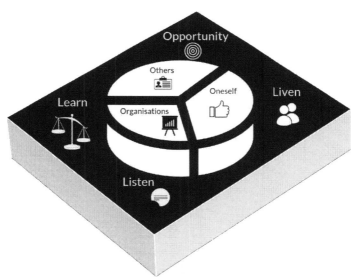

THE **LOS** Model ™

Many times I come across LinkedIn profile statuses stating that the individual is 'looking for the next opportunity' especially if the person is coming out of the military. This defies the purpose of opportunity, and also raises a few questions. How do you find opportunity? Does opportunity find you? Is it luck?

Well let's first define opportunity:

'A time or set of circumstances that makes it possible to do something.'

Merriam Webster goes further to say:

'When a person gets the chance to do something he or she wants to do.'

So opportunity is not luck, because if it is you will be able to take it when it knocks. You need to be ready when opportunity knocks. If not, then opportunity will pass you by.

After years of looking at opportunity and trying to define it, here is the best way to describe it: "You are the opportunity."

In 1999, my dad passed away at the early age of 49. Since he had done over 29 years of service in the Mauritius Police Force, my mum was entitled to a pension which was, at the time, quite a substantial sum of money. As a widow, it was enough money to keep my mum from having to work. She put it in an investment and lived on the interest. I was 24 years old at the time, living in Mauritius, and I was the main breadwinner for the house bills and my sister. I asked my mum if she would help me pay for my flight to London and I would repay her, and she agreed. So there I was in enrolled in one of the most reputable CIM (Chartered Institute of Marketing) courses in the heart of London. Naturally, I had to find a job to support myself and my family. My first job was as a porter/dish washer at Buckingham Palace. I have to admit that I have no idea how I got that job or how my friend got me this job after simply filling out a few forms. When you are from the Commonwealth, born in Mauritius, you know quite a lot about the royal family and the United Kingdom as part of the school curriculum. You see that some roads are painted red: red roads are not a common colour from where I come from. You see the guards and it is quite a scene, like living in Disneyland, these days. It was an exciting day for me when Her Majesty came around to thank all of us and I got to see her – and I'd only been in London for two weeks. This revived my childhood ambition to be in the military, like my uncles who were in the Special Forces in Mauritius. So my attention turned to the police officers in the control room and military guards. They looked the part, seriously ready for action, which prompted me to have a good conversation with one of the armed police officers. Now I have a lot of respect for police officers: I grew up among them in the married quarter when I was growing up, and always saw them as the good guys. So, this has always been with me. This officer told me that unfortunately, to become a police officer you needed to have lived a certain length of time in the country and perhaps even hold British nationality, but that the military was more open to Commonwealth applicants. I knew he was right because my grandfather served in the British Army during World War Two in North Africa.

Would you say the above was luck? I don't think so. If I hadn't taken a leap of faith, with the support and blessing of my mum and sister, I would still be a freeport officer at the Mauritius Freeport Authority, working in parallel with the Mauritius customs and excise department at the port and airport under a free trade agreement for import and export of goods and services. Life was good, we were doing ok – but was ok good enough?

After years of studying the subject, I have come to the realisation that you create opportunity – you are the opportunity, opportunity looks you in the face each and every time you get frustrated with your boss, each time you get fired, each time you are at the end of your contract. When circumstances present themselves, see the opportunity in them.

My mum paying for my flight has been the greatest investment she could ever have made for me.

So from now on, each time you are faced with a work decision, see it as an opportunity, look it in the eye and be ready to embrace it and make the jump. Landing in London with no fixed address, no job, and a limited amount of money, I saw opportunity everywhere. Even nowadays, when I see a homeless person begging near Victoria train station with a can of coke next to him and a lit cigarette in his hand, talking on his mobile phone, I think to myself, 'This person is so lucky to be in London.' I cannot imagine this same person in Africa or India.

Like Tony J. Selimi, who was once homeless on the streets of London, living on just £2 a day: he is now a best-selling author and international speaker. I interviewed Errol Lawson, who is an entrepreneur, author, pastor and life coach. At fifteen he was part of a drug squad, homeless, lost and his next opportunity was going to be jail. However, he turned his life around completely, reinventing himself by the age of 25. He is now a well-respected man, sought after as a John Maxwell coach, travelling the world teaching others how to change their lives. There are many other people we will be discussing in this book as we go along, but the one thing which remains the same is that each and every one of those people saw themselves as the opportunity.

If opportunity equals options, then look at your options. Just recently I saw an old mate of mine who is still serving in the Forces and had to have knee surgery. I took an afternoon off to go see him and after a few minutes reminiscing about our time when we were serving, the conversation turned to his future with the military. It is sad but unless he makes a full recovery, this knee injury could impact his career progression for promotion, or even staying in the military. This can be, and has been, a shocking moment, resulting in the end of term for many. But this could also be opportunity knocking, the perfect time to reinvent himself. We took a look at his options and how to make the best of it, enjoy more time with his family and look at a possible new career. In the corporate world, I see a lot of potentially extremely successful people frustrated by their jobs, and leaders who most likely can do a better job than their boss. But I also see fear, and I see people looking for the easy way to bring home a salary.

I have come across a lot of people who completely make the wrong career decision purely because they allow so much fear to build up inside them at the time of transition that they choose the easy way out. I had the same fear, doubt and concern when I decided to change career in the British Armed Forces and nearly became a victim of fear when I took my first job as an HGV driver. The pay matched my military pay and even allowed me some saving on the side. Working hours were fixed. It was comfortable.

"We all have fear, fear of failure, fear of loss, fear of heights, fear of public speaking but when fear stops you from trying anything else then you have a problem."

The problem becomes more apparent in times of a career change, especially when you have dependants or peer pressure. I looked for a replacement salary when I took my lorry driving job and if you let fear control you, you end up in a cage.

During my LOS podcast, I do a series of talks with industry leaders from the three main generations: the baby boomers, gen x and millennials. One of the questions I always ask them is:

'What would you have done differently in your leadership career if you could go back?' The answer I get every time is: 'Take more risks and ignore fear'.

As an entrepreneur, fear is also present every time you make a business decision, as you think about the impact on the business and other people.

One of the greatest men in history to face his fear is Abraham Lincoln, who was born into poverty and faced adversity throughout his life. Lincoln lost eight elections, failed twice in business and suffered a nervous breakdown. He could have quit many times due to fear but he didn't. Facing his fears allowed him to become one of the greatest presidents in the history of the United States of America.

Other industry leaders who faced their fear, regardless of the situation, would be Nelson Mandela and Mahatma Gandhi.

Both had to take a substantial risk to face what they stood for to the very end. It didn't just change our lives for a few years, it affected our outlook on the world.

I am a firm believer that if you do those things that are easy, life becomes hard, but if you do things that are hard, life gets easy. It is easy to stay in a job you don't like, easy not to exercise, easy to keep smoking, easy to eat unhealthy food, easy to stay in the status quo. Look at the terrible impact these things make in your life. You get sick, die sooner, and die unsatisfied with your life.

Here is an interesting observation to this chapter:

'Opportunity is nowhere' – what can you see in these letters?

I see the words: 'Opportunity is now here!'

We are in the digital age, where you just need to open your phone to see the things you like, want, need and desire, but you can also see it as the time to step into that next role, claim that role you have long been waiting for, and reinvent yourself into that perfect work-life balance role. We will look at the options and the human skills that are likely to become automated and how you have to think outside the box in the next chapter.

Here are my 7 action steps to seek opportunity:

1. Look for it and start from where you are; at your workplace, your clients and your contacts.
2. Get out and meet new people. Buy them a coffee and share ideas.
3. Never burn bridges.
4. Be a giver, and find ways to bring value to people's lives. In doing so, it will lift you up.
5. Know you are most probably sitting on a mountain of opportunity.
6. Stop feeding your mind with negative thoughts.
7. You are the opportunity, so find yourself.

Leavers to Leaders Lead Opportunity

Think outside the box and with the end in mind

In Southampton where I live, we have around 500 cruise ships visiting us each year. Being a turnaround port, these ships carry about 2,500 to 4,500 passengers each, with a ratio of 1:3 for the crew on average. So, around 2 million visitors and 450,000 crew members per year. The itinerary for those ships is prepared years in advance, as the cruise company has to book the berthing, arrange for resupply, transportation, fresh crew and more. This is logistics at its best.

At each stage of this logistics planning, there is a contingency plan for when things do not go according to plan. Things go wrong and ships miss their port of call, and there are delays due to adverse weather. So when setting off, the ship officer is constantly updating his reports on the weather and mechanical engineers are at work 24/7 for the smooth running of this ship. How is all of this relevant to you as a leaver in transition, and how do you leverage all these as opportunities? It is by thinking outside the box, and being like the cruise industry and always having a contingency plan.

You see, nothing goes according to plan in life. You cannot predict the next hour even if you are at home, on the road, or in the workplace. Things are constantly changing, same as things constantly change for a cruise ship miles away from land. While sailing away, especially if the ship is doing a transatlantic sailing which takes about 10 days, people need to be fed, the engines have to work at their best, staff need to rest and the voyage needs to end on a good note for the 2,500 passengers.

> *"It is all about having a plan, a plan that gives you a direction, an aim and a focus."*

This plan needs to be built with the aim of being able to readjust, if necessary. There is no point in having a set plan with a set aim. A plan needs to be flexible so it can be realigned, the same way a cruise ship will readjust according to the weather or any problem on board. I am constantly telling military personnel to have a few plans, but most importantly to have a failing plan, a catastrophic plan, for themselves and their families. The job they are paid to do is constantly changing, and the risk is far greater than normal day-to-day living. There have been more killed by friendly fire than killed in action during the war in Iraq and Afghanistan. My advice to military personnel is to start planning your exit the day you enlist. Take career decisions, including training and courses that will help with your exit. I can promise you if you are not thinking with the end in mind (and I am talking about your career ending) your future is in danger.

In the 2016 report from the *World Economic Forum – The Future of Jobs* refers to the-change in the industries with a fourth industrial revolution: how developments in genetics, artificial intelligence, robotics, nanotechnology, 3D printing and biotechnology, to name just a few, are all building on and amplifying one another.

The report goes on to say how this growing change is likely to create not only mass employment but also new jobs, and how you need to constantly be re-skilling and up-scaling. The survey and research resulted in an extensive list of talents and strategies for leading global employers, representing more than 13 million employees across 9 broad industry sectors in 15 major developed and emerging economies and regional economic areas.[2] The report looked at the impact already felt, and future impact by other demographic and socio-economic factors such as: the changing nature of work, flexible work, the middle class in emerging markets, climate change, natural resources, geopolitical volatility, consumer ethics, privacy issues, longevity, ageing societies, young demographics in emerging markets, women's economic power, aspirations, and rapid urbanisation. These are some of the reasons why you need to be constantly mindful of your future and to remember that transition is upon us.

Another report by Scott McLeod and Karl Fisch addressed how much needs to be done in educating the future generation, as 65% of those entering education today will be facing a completely different job market, with jobs that don't yet exist.[3] These reports are alarming to me, as I still have three young daughters at school and I am concerned for their future. In the light of all this evidence, you need to be able to think outside the box and plan your future and get ready for your transition. I

---

[2] http://www3.weforum.org/docs/WEF_Future_of_Jobs.pdf
[3] McLeod, Scott and Karl Fisch, "Shift Happens", https://shifthappens.wikispaces.com.

have no doubt that even my companies will have to face the challenges described above. We will look at those in more depth in some of the other chapters. As I write this chapter I am also very mindful of service leavers who are trained to think outside the box and be prepared for Plan B. This is why I am a strong advocate that military personnel in transition have the best skillset to reinvent and retrain and become a leader. This chapter is a tribute to them.

Having a clear vision is a valuable function as a leaver in transition. Not only do you need to think of the long-term impact but also the short-term consequences and from there you build a strategy to get to your destination. As I left Mauritius in 2001, I had a clear goal and my goal was to gain more experience, educate myself and find a better life. I was however prepared for anything, even returning to Mauritius, which is why I took two years leave without pay from my old job, an option when you worked for a government organisation in Mauritius. Was it my Plan B? I didn't yet know the importance of having a Plan C or D, but it was there.

> *"Get into the habit to have a vision and a few plans A, B, C and D."*

The future beyond 2020 does require it. A vision for a better, more effective lifestyle is a good start. But to make it work well, you also need to have a clear vision of yourself in the future. Have you ever done a jigsaw puzzle or seen someone doing one? How important is it to have the final scene is mind?

3   HOW IMPORTANT IS IT, THE FINAL SCENE OF THE FUTURE?!

When your destination is clear, you can keep coming back to the ship's itinerary again and again and update your ETA for the next port of call. This brings us to the next important skill you need as you navigate in the open seas: your compass.

We will cover this in the next chapter but let's look at the 7 steps to help you think outside the box:

1. Be open-minded to change. Clearly we all know that change is already here.
2. Think win-win. Always place yourself in a position when both parties win.
3. Step outside your comfort zone, we will be repeating this over and over.
4. Take time off to think of your future of work, because I can promise you no one else will.
5. Have the end in mind.
6. Be prepared to change course but have your destination in mind.
7. Add value to your community, workplace and be a person of value.

Leavers to Leaders Lead Opportunity

Discover your Compass

You know your destination and you have a vision, but things change. How do you know if you are still heading in the same direction? We call this setting your compass. The 7 steps to reinvent yourself from a leaver to a leader is a framework that puts you in control of your own life in a creative way, using your own life experiences. With this, you can become a creative force to reinvent yourself in your current workplace. So the first purpose of this book is to help you recognise your inner force – your compass – that will be an inner guidance system of the L.O.S (Leaders' Operating System) that will help you stay on track as you move towards your destination.

I often enjoy meeting up with some of our leaders and see their eyes sparkling as we engage in the type of training and workshops we run at TriExForces which in itself is a combination of a travel and a training company. Our workshops trifecta on Leading Oneself, Leading Others and Leading Organisation, which I called the 3LOS. I personally take great pleasure in planning with my team and designing those programmes and itineraries. As I live near the sea and with Southampton being the main capital with one of my businesses in the cruise industry, I often see cruise agents advertising for a "cruise to nowhere". Maybe you've been on one. The journey is simple. Instead of the ship leaving for some adventurous or exotic places, it goes out at sea and travels in circle, while the passengers all enjoy some great shows, and activities onboard. A cruise to nowhere may be a fun way to spend a few days, but it's no way to spend your life. The whole idea of cruising is to explore places and experience new things.

The same applies to your own compass, and if you don't set a compass, you will be going on a cruise to nowhere. You will stay in the same boring job, have the same annoying boss and unfortunately earn the same wage until your job is disrupted and you become a leaver in transition. Let's face it, ten years on since the 2008 recession, many people's lives changed, but for most, life has either remained the same or got worse. Living costs have gone up while wages have been stagnating. And having had a close look at the last 10 years, earnings have lagged behind prices of food, utilities and housing costs for most of the decade since the start of the recession. In the public sector, a pay freeze (from 2011) and pay cap (from 2013) kept wage rises below inflation, while in the private sector wage growth has also been slow.

Unfortunately this behaviour also exists in the military. I have come across service personnel who have been in the same rank for years and have no intention of going anywhere. The military has a rank structure second to none which has been in use for centuries, and tested by years of wars and conflicts. It is designed for you to grow and not get comfortable. You need to identify and set sail toward your destination. In other words, you need to discover your dream, and you need to find the time to discover your internal compass that will take you to your dream. The whole secret of transitioning is to find out what is your destiny and your passion and to make a plan to accomplish it. Then do it.

One of my heroes since I was 14 years old is the celebrity, Arnold Schwarzenegger. His dream grew out of body building. He was the world's best body builder for six consecutive years. From boyhood, he had a passion for studying the anatomy. He taught himself how to train, and then he went to the USA to train as a professional, and became a movie star due to his physique. He became known, liked and trusted as the Governor of California from 2003 to 2011. He has an internal compass that has set him for years as an Austrian-American actor, filmmaker, businessman, investor, author, philanthropist, activist, politician, and former professional bodybuilder and powerlifter.

Setting your compass will help you understand how far you have to go and help you identify where you are. The British Army has a huge rank structure from Private to Warrant Officer class one. One is expected have reached the top rank by the time they are about to retire, others do cross over to the officer's rank if they are ambitious enough and have set their compass high enough. Will your compass help you to know how far you need to go?

When I was 11 years old, we used to live in a city called Vacoas, which is very green and in the high land. The back of our house was surrounded by mountains and some hills with sugar cane plantations leading from our land to the mountain. I somehow knew the sea was behind those mountains and I wished you could just climb on top of the house to see it. One school holiday I set off to go and see the sea, which meant I was going to climb this mountain. No one knew about it; not my friends nor my parents. Early that morning, I set off with a bottle of water and after walking for one hour, I found myself at the foot of this huge and colossal mountain called Trois Mammelles – French for Three Peaks. There was no coming back: my dream was on the other side of this mountain if I wanted to see the ocean.

4.. "FOLLOW YOUR DREAM,...YOU CAN ACHIEVE IT IF YOU SEE IT!!"
((ANYTHING IS POSSIBLE IF YOU BELIEVE IN YOURSELF!!))
WHEN!!!

It was not an easy climb, but clearly others had been there before me as the tracks leading to the top indicated. After much work, I reached the middle first peak and I could barely recognise my own house, but the sad part was that the ocean was not on the other side. I could see it in the distance and figured it was maybe another two hours' walk. My compass was set to see the ocean, and I did, I also learned about distance and the time it takes to cover it.

At the age of 15, I discovered a road track around the mountain and sugar cane that took me to the ocean in 15 minutes – going downhill at some crazy speed. I remember escaping to the sea a lot. Getting there was easy, but coming back would need the determination and courage to face the hill, trying to avoid getting told off by my dad for going away without permission.

Finding your internal compass is not as hard as you think. It may even be staring you in the face. Your compass is your master key and when you find it you are on a journey. This is the premise of 'Leavers to Leaders'.

During my interview with Errol Lawson, author *of* '5 Core Abilities of Highly Effective Leaders', he told me he discovered his ambition to become a leader as a child, but he went the wrong way about it. Errol is now an inspirational coach for teenagers: a well-known figure in the city of Birmingham for leading the young community.

So here are 7 steps to help you discover your internal compass:

1. Ask people who know you – you will be surprised how much others know about you.
2. Take time out to examine yourself. Steal one hour a week of your busy life to do this.
3. Read about the life of other people who may have had the same problem as you, and if possible, reach out to them.
4. Study your life so far. Go back as far as when you were 10 years old. What can you remember?
5. What is the one thing your colleagues, boss, friends and family say about you?
6. Face your fears and do it anyway.
7. Remember the past is not an indication of your future.

Leavers to Leaders Lead Opportunity

Evaluate

No one knows your career situation like you do. You are the one in charge of your ship, dealing with the turbulence, the weather, the forces that would affect you and put your personal life off track. You are the one most equipped to understand what needs to happen in your career, and to make it happen. Far more than techniques and practices that may have worked in other situations, you need to have an approach that will enable and empower you.

This is where self-evaluation comes into play.

Before you begin, you must hit the pause button.

5 "EMBRACE CHANGE!... √16 ACCELERATING"

When you hit the pause button you are able to take a deep and long look at yourself. In a modern day where things are constantly changing and the rate of change is accelerating, you need to anchor yourself with some solid ground and then embrace this change.

Around 2001, when I wanted to reinvent myself, I had a few options at hand. The first option was to move to Australia, the second option was to move to Canada and the third option was London. As it turned out, after evaluating my options, I knew little about Australia or Canada, but London was very well known in Mauritius. As a former British colony we had been ruled by the British from 1810 to 1968 and a lot of the stability and economy is due to the solid structure and national constitution established by the British. To this day, our law enforcement and police force have grounded roots from the British military. Evaluating your position is one of the most important assessments you can take. An honest approach to self-evaluation is worth a million pounds.

When you are on a pause, there are 3 things you are able to do and they are:

Self awareness, self-consciousness, and your independent will.

As a leaver wishing to become a leader, you need to be able to think strategically about your future so that you can deal with change by being more proactive and not reactive. You need to use the change driven by technology, education, equipment and organisation to advance yourself. As a leaver, you need to lead change. The military is an environment where change is inevitable, and they have handled change well in the past and will continue to do so in the future. The military helps its personnel to anticipate change by seeking to continuously improve. Right from the beginning, after your have successfully completed your military training, you have no idea where you will be posted until a few weeks before your graduation, (known as a pass-out parade). In some cases depending on your role, you are posted for a maximum of three years, with no idea where your next posting will be. You, as a future leader, need to become self aware of your environment.

6, KNOW YOUR VALUE!!

Being conscious is a style that allows you to take advantage of your skills and existing knowledge and experience. I often come across potential leaders who have been in key positions for years but are unlikely to make it to the next level. Maybe you are comfortable, maybe you are scared or even cannot see very clearly. A conscious approach will put you in the spotlight, you will see yourself and you will become more aware of who you really are. I can guarantee, no one else can be more conscious of you than yourself.

Sometimes you may need someone to help you see the mountain of value that you are already sitting on, which perhaps even your peers and your boss are well aware of. They know the business will tip if you were to leave the workplace tomorrow. When thinking about your value, watch out for the following signs.

Have you returned from a holiday and your work colleagues are relieved to see you on your return? Or has the workload been shifted and has work just gone on as usual? These are signs of what I call being a vital person or a functional person. We will look into this in more detail later in this book as we talk about leading the organisation in Chapter 7.

Now that you are aware of you, imagine your potential. Would your current place of work fall into pieces if you were to leave? What value do you bring? Imagine how it will look for you to be in control of a vital part of your workplace and lead others — would you still be in this same workplace? Would it be fun to work? Are you afraid to be asked, "Why do we do it this way?" These are some of the evaluating questions you must ask as you steer yourself to being a leader. You need to independently put yourself out there by using the current opportunities available to you.

Here are 7 tips to help you evaluate yourself in your current workplace:

1. Be ready to evaluate yourself at least quarterly. Big businesses have quarterly reviews, and so should you.
2. Question the environment or industry you are currently in. Do they want to change, or adopt new strategies in light of a digital revolution?
3. Get into the habit of thinking first and acting later to change your reaction.
4. Act your way to new thinking.
5. Stop being a follower and start being a leader.
6. Look at who you are surrounded by. Most of the time we tend to surround ourselves with people we are comfortable with.
7. How important are you in your organisation?

Richard Booth's
BOOKSHOP ✦ CAFÉ ✦ CINEMA
Est. 1962

Richard Booth's idea
that a town full of books could
become an international
attraction, transformed the
small market community of
Hay-on-Wye into the world's
first book town.

This landmark bookshop
on Lion Street extends over

Second Hand & New Books
Bought & Sold

✦

Literature

✦

History

✦

Children's

✦

Topography

✦

Natural History

✦

Theology

✦

Science

✦

Art & Music

✦

Humour

✦

Modern Languages

✦

Classics

✦

Anglo Welsh

✦

Science Fiction

✦

and more...

CHAPTER 2

Leavers to Leaders Liven Up Others

Never Leave People the Same Way You Found Them

Is it not fascinating that no humans are identical, not even identical twins? Let's take for example fingerprints, which police officers use to identify one person from another. They can do this because we all have unique fingerprints. Fingerprints are not the only difference, nor are they the most important. Each one of us is unique in many other ways, hence why twins, even though they have same DNA, have different fingerprints. Much like having your own unique fingerprints, you have your own skills, talents, abilities, and ideas.

Time and again, I come across people in work positions who really don't care. Especially if you are the face of the business, our eyes are attracted to movement, and being animated when you speak will make people more interested in you. This is why it is important to give the people you come across at work your full focus, your full attention.

Appear focused. Do this well, and you will find that people become more interested in you. You don't need to have a pretty or fresh face, people can tell if you are genuine. Your future is in your first impression. Your customers at work, your peers may not remember your skills, but they will never forget how you made them feel when interacting with you.

What matters is expression and focus. The same way that emojis have become a certain way to communicate, and express ourselves, there are different tones of emoji out there. Emoji is derived from emotion. You need to use this in your own facial expressions to make it easier for others to focus on you when you speak. It is not just about emoji, is it about responding to funny, sad, shocked, surprised faces.

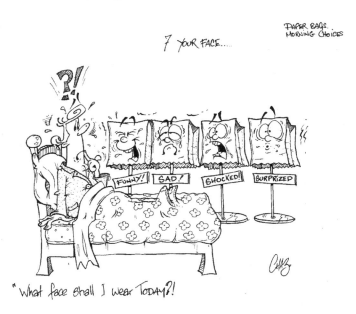

" What face shall I wear Today?!

> *"Your face is the window to your soul.*
> *People respond to emotion."*

We will look at the soul in terms of spirit later in this book, and how it is important to know that your outside is a reflection of your inside.

Be open to others who are different from you when seeking out new people. You do not want all your friends and colleagues to be your clones. You will not be able to share, trade or learn with someone who is a clone. Understand that the more different you are, the more you will be able to benefit from one another. Differences allow us to communicate and exchange knowledge and wisdom. If we had nothing to learn from each other, what would it be like? The only reason we can liven up others is because we are different. So celebrate difference. I could say I am lucky enough to be born in Mauritius, an island that is so diverse from origin that none of us are the same. In 1800, the French invaded Mauritius and brought plantation workers from India, China, Africa and Asia. They were all so different from each other that they couldn't talk to each other. Since their masters spoke French, they found it easier to copy them, which gave birth to a new language 'Creole' – a sort of broken French. To this day we speak French, Creole, Hindi, Mandarin, Urdu, Tamil and British English. When you land in Mauritius, apart from the tropical setting and white sandy beaches, the first thing that catches your eyes is the diversity of culture. We are blessed to have access to all the best food in the world and enjoy each other's cultures which we gained from our ancestors. As I wrote this section, I realised I know very little about my origin, although I was told that 'The Reddy' came from South India and it is my mission to not only trace back my origin but also work in India. This book will cover more on managing diversity in the workplace which is a key aspect nowadays, with the multi-generation of baby boomers, generation x and millennials.

This is why it is so glorious to be human at this present time. This is why each time you meet someone, you have the ability to influence him or her. Hence why leadership works: it allows us to trade in what we don't have. I can do things that you can't, you can do things that I can't. But if we trade, we can actually enjoy each other's abilities. In this way, we are able to help one another as we help ourselves.

Why is 'livening up others' so important?

As a leader you will constantly be faced with people and their problems. Either they will come to you with their troubles or you will become aware all is not well and that something must be done about it. These people will come to you as they feel close enough and professionally secure enough to share their troubles with you. My dad was a great counsellor, I remember people stopping him on the road to seek advice. These were people from different backgrounds and cultures, but he as a police officer was able to advise them professionally. I remember a story he told about a man he met at a bus stop on his way to work. It was a rainy day, so my dad invited him to share his umbrella and they started talking. They talked a bit more on the bus. A few days later, he came across that same man during a police investigation. At that time, my dad was a detective sergeant in Port Louis Harbour, the capital of Mauritius.

I remember my dad saying it was very difficult to see clearly on this case and he had to ask his subordinate to be the judge. I never really understood this situation; how did it matter that he had offered shelter to this man? Later, I learned that doing a favour for somebody else causes you to like him or her more. My dad knew it would be wrong to handle such an investigation because he would show favour to the man he had helped. Dad may have been subconsciously biased toward him, so it was right to withdraw from this investigation.

"Because the truth is, we love those whom we help more than those who help us."

The same principle will apply as we give rather than receive, because, as the saying in the Bible goes, "there is more happiness in giving than in receiving." [4]

Begin to implement this strategy and technique today, it will pay infinite dividends in your personal and professional life.

---

[4] Acts 20:35

So here are the 7 actions to help you liven up others:

1. Be genuine when interacting with others.
2. Learn to know people better and work to understand them.
3. Use facial expressions when talking.
4. Become more energetic when you talk with others.
5. Pay attention to your body language: don't cross your arms, or look around or look at your phone when talking with people.
6. Spend time with people.
7. Remember it is more fun to give than receive.

Leavers to Leaders Liven Up Others

Passion

Growing up in the 80s, I heard the word 'holiday' a lot. I have also met a lot of people from all around the world travelling to Mauritius for their dream holiday. To this day, the island attracts around 1.3 million tourists a year and has a population of 1.2 million. But growing up, we never had a holiday as we would describe it nowadays. As a nation, we have always been very good at hosting others, but I think this is changing. It certainly changed for me. When I meet people, they get to know me and my place of birth, and they all seem to have Mauritius on their bucket list as a holiday destination. Now as Mauritian-British, I completely understand it.

But when I was 21 years old, after working for three years as an officer for the Mauritius Freeport Authority under the directive of Gerard Sanspeur, the CEO at the time, I witnessed hundreds and maybe thousands of goods from China and Africa transiting through the Mauritius free zone. So my best friend Yannick and I decided to travel to China and Hong Kong to see the world of import and export. The following year we travelled to another country for a different reason, which resulted in us starting our first business together. Funnily enough, it wasn't an import and export business but a dog breeding business. We both owned Great Danes, and after attending a few dog shows around the world, we started our first business. If you are not familiar with

Great Danes then think of a small horse, as you can sit on this dog. This breed requires lots of walks and exercise and also a lot of attention. After the first mating, we had 11 pups and we sold all of them, and we then for some crazy reason bought a St Bernard pup originating from Belgium for our next breed. Unfortunately I was not there to see the St Bernard pups, as two years later I flew to London – that was in 2001.

During all this time I had a passion which I didn't understand until later, I loved travelling, seeing the world, meeting different people, eating different foods, and wearing different clothes while doing business. My passion is about mixing work and travelling. Unfortunately, it took me a long time to figure this out. My point is that as you move from a leaver to a leader, spend time finding your passion. The best definition of passion I have come across is from the Collins English Dictionary:

Passion is a very strong feeling about something or a strong belief in something. [5]

But passion on its own is not enough. There has to be something more and that something more is grit, which is best described here:

In contrast, grit is argued to be a trait of perseverance. Grit enables an individual to persevere in accomplishing a goal despite obstacles over an extended period. When compared with the construct of persistence, grit adds a component of

---

[5] https://www.collinsdictionary.com/dictionary/english/passion

passion for the goal.[6]

8.

"GRIT ENABLES AN INDIVIDUAL TO PERSERVER IN ACCOMPLISHING AN OBSTACLES
TO ACHIEVE THE PASSION TO REACH THE GOAL!"

I have very often met with people who started out full of energy and enthusiasm about a new job, a new prospect or even a new promotion, only to then find out two years later that same flame has died.

I recently gave a lecture on passion in the local community where I live in Southampton, United Kingdom. After the session, two young undergraduates approached me with their exciting business plan for the 70,000 plus students of Southampton, which I could see was interesting as well. After listening to their stories, I suggested we talk again in one year, so I could see where they were at. I do the same for all new entrepreneurs who come up with fresh ideas, simply because

---

[6] https://en.wikipedia.org/wiki/Grit_(personality_trait)

most have the great idea but what I am looking for is the endurance, the grit, the passion.

During a short discussion with Theo Paphitis, former BBC Dragons' Den entrepreneur, while he was at Solent University of Southampton, he encouraged me to find my passion and shared how his passion had got him in his life and in business.

Later on that same year, I caught up with my friend, Yannick, on Facebook. He was in Mauritius, his home base between other parts of Africa and Australia where he runs his business. After reminiscing about our work and trading news about our children, I asked Yannick to reflect back on the idea of passion and how it had played out in our lives. We both agreed that we wanted to travel and do business, have sit-down meals with serious people and discuss business, and that's exactly what we are both doing now. We agreed that our passion for dogs is still the same, but unfortunately since we are both extremely busy running our businesses around the world, perhaps it is best for us to leave it to our children. But then again, our main passion has never been about dogs!

I have unfortunately wasted a lot of time looking, thinking and searching for my passion in the past. Don't make the same mistake: take time off to find your passion. This could mean stealing an hour a week, or a week a year, to focus on finding what really moves you, then set yourself a goal to achieve it.

So now we know that if you have a passion then you need grit to persevere to accomplish a goal. Passion on its own is not enough, especially when you face hardship. On your way to becoming a leader, you need both passion and grit. Sometimes your passion may not be very clear. I couldn't really see mine when I started travelling, so sometimes you may need to be surrounded by people who can help you find it. Again, consider Arnold Schwarzenegger and his passion for body building. He was born in 1947, a year of famine, and at twenty-one years old he was in Los Angeles and crowned Mr Universe. At twenty six, he was the greatest body builder in the world, and by 36 he had a college degree and was a millionaire. By forty seven he was one of the world's biggest movie stars, and by fifty seven he was elected Governor of California. His passion and grit was so strong that it stayed with him for thirty-six years.

I have developed a programme which can help you identify where you are on your leadership journey based on the seven steps described in this book. The result of the scorecard is based on certain questions and gives you a customised report of where you are and where you need to improve to reinvent yourself as a leader: www.LeaversToLeaders.com/scorecard. Please pause your reading and have a go at this online test.

When you come back, you can look at the 7 ways to find your passion:

1. Be open-minded when you meet up with others.
2. Engage with people out of your circle. Read about them, and if you can, reach out to them.
3. Take a break from work, spend time with your loved ones while finding out what moves you.
4. Ask people close to you to describe you. You will be surprised at how much they know about you.
5. Get comfortable being uncomfortable around others.
6. Take a leap of faith, believe in yourself.
7. Remember the future is now. You can start becoming the leader you always wanted to be regardless of your field of expertise and industry.

Leavers to Leaders Liven Up Others

Be The Best

My first interaction with the military was with the British Army. I remember walking via The Strand after work one evening at Buckingham Palace to catch Bus 29 to Seven Sisters. Outside, on the wall at the front of the building was a sign which read, 'Army: Be The Best'. This simple sign had three powerful words: BE THE BEST. I was familiar with ISO 9002 and other standard measurement tools but these three words had more power than an ISO 9002 for me. I joined the military and became the best, so naturally when I founded TriExForces, I wanted something that would resonate with me and the value this brand would deliver, so we used the words, 'TO SERVE'. Since our team is made up from former service personnel and blue light services, serving has got to be the main thing that we have in common as leavers from those services. By serving others, we become the best.

In this chapter I want to stretch your imagination to how to be the best. What does it take to be the best?

Henry Ford, Andrew Carnegie, David Ogilvy, Michael Jordan, Bill Gates, Thomas J Watson, Warren Buffet, Steve Job, Elon Musk and Arnold Schwarzenegger all reveal major fascinating details and traits about themselves, their character and personalities as they educate, enlighten, and entertain us with often surprising views, but through it all they are always the best at what they do. When Arnold set off from Austria in 1968 to America, he had one thing in mind and that was to be the strongest man in the world. He went on to win Mr Olympia seven times. Between 1980 to 1990, he worked hard, took acting classes to get into Hollywood and he did just that, and created some of the best movies that are still valid even now. He went on to become the first Austrian-American Governor of California. If it was not for his desire and work ethic to be the best in life, Arnold would not be who he is today.

Bill Gates, back in the 80s, said during an interview that in the age of information, communication will flow digitally over email so we can act on news with flexible speed. We will be studying sales data to find patterns and insights of the customers' behaviours and we will be using digital tools to create virtual teams that can share knowledge and build on each other's ideas in real time, worldwide. Paper will be converted into a digital process to eliminate administrative bottleneck which will free up knowledge workers for more important work. All of the above are now here and, if you are to succeed and become a leader for the next 5 to 10 years, you need to be able to be better than a machine. To be better and smarter than machine means we must use skills that machines cannot copy. What are those skills?

Communication is everywhere. Open LinkedIn, someone is communicating either by written or spoken words. It is the same with all other social mediums. The world is busy with communication. But this is not the type of communication I am talking about. I am talking about the ability to communicate *effectively*. To be the best, you need to know when to write a text or an email and when to pick up the phone and have a conversation. I made a huge mistake a few years back. At that time, I was the executive director at Glenn Arekion Ministries, an outreach organisation based in Louisville, Kentucky. Rather than picking up the phone to address a problem, I sent an email. I have known Glenn for a while but we still relate to this event as a miscommunication. Understand that written words can easily be misinterpreted. For example, can you think what would happen if you meant to say to your loved one, 'What's wrong?' but instead you said 'What's wrong with you?' The latter will generate a very different reaction, one which may end with you being in the dog house!

9. WHAT'S WRONG WITH YOU... CAN END UP WITH YOU BEING IN THE DOG HOUSE!?

When you learn to communicate effectively, it means you have the receiving person's best interests at heart. When you have the best interests of the other person at heart, you think before you act, you think before you talk, you think before you write. If you wish to express your views and they are negative, write them down, use your voice recorder and get it out of your system. Then listen back to it and if you still think the other person needs to hear it, then fire away.

Being the best means being the best in all senses. Physically, my best time was at the age of 22 when it took me 7.30 minutes to run 1.5 miles and I could curl a 40kg barbell. Now I do less on the run, probably because I am out of practice, but I can still curl 40kg at my best.

So here is a little exercise for you to complete:

I ……… (your name) aim to be the best (son, daughter, husband, wife, partner, boyfriend, girlfriend, dad, mum, friend, colleague, co-worker, business partner and leader). Then watch the world around you change as you discover yourself and liven up those around you.

As I say: be the best and discover yourself.

Here are my 7 steps to being the best:

1. Communicate effectively with words.
2. Go to bed and examine your day.
3. React quickly when you made a mistake.
4. Write or voice record your most unwanted feelings.
5. Have the best interests of the receiver at heart.
6. Don't become a perfectionist, no one is perfect.
7. Surround yourself with good people who positively influence your life.

CHAPTER 3

Leavers to Leaders Listen to Others

Listen to Understand, Not to Respond

This chapter is all about the art of listening. Don't you find it interesting that we have two ears and one mouth? It would be weird the other way around, but listening to others is one of the best ways to educate yourself and let this become an art as a leader.

The author Stephen R. Covey once said that the biggest problem with communication is we listen to reply and not to understand. Listening is a skill that we develop from the womb and typically it is called discriminative listening. As adults, we still use this skill – especially if you are in a foreign place where you can distinguish between the voice of a male or female, or even an upset or happy tone of a voice. To become a leader, your interpersonal skills must become a crucial part of your existence. How many times have you heard that people quit not because of their jobs, but because of their leaders? The Deloitte report in 2015 on UK Talent for Survival highlighted that knowledge is no more a valuable skill in the future, nor are technical and digital skills as important, but are specialisms required by only a minority of workers. Programming skills or technology design skills are important to five per cent of the workforce or less.

<blockquote>10. "WE LISTEN TO REPLY,..SOMETIMES WITHOUT UNDERSTANDING !?"</blockquote>

The number one ranking in the future talent report is the cognitive ability to listen to and understand information and ideas presented through spoken words and sentences.[7]

This is why I have dedicated a whole chapter to why listening skills are fundamental for anyone looking to become a leader beyond 2020.

---

[7] https://www2.deloitte.com/content/dam/Deloitte/uk/Documents/Growth/deloitte-uk-talent-for-survival-report.pdf

Let's start with the three types of listening. Let us explore them one by one and understand which form is most relevant to a leader. You may also find out that these skills are also very important at home. Just recently, my daughters realised I have been lacking attention when they talked with me, and when this became apparent to them they started using it to get the best deal out of me rather than my wife. So I am often told, 'Daddy you are not listening, look at me,' which I did, giving them my full attention. These simple words of command were very effective. Yet even as adults, we tend to forget or become lazy at paying attention when someone is talking to us.

Whenever you listen, learn something and become engaged in informational listening. This is true in many day-to-day situations, in education and at work: when you listen to the news, watch a documentary, when a friend tells you a recipe or when you are talked through a technical problem with a computer. There are many other examples of informational listening too. Although all types of listening are 'active' – they require concentration and a conscious effort to understand. Informational listening is less active than many of the other types of listening. When we're listening to learn or be instructed we are taking in new information and facts; we are not criticising or analysing. Informational listening, especially in formal settings like in work meetings or while in education, is often accompanied by note taking – a way of recording key information so that it can be reviewed later.

We can be said to be engaged in critical listening when the goal is to evaluate or scrutinise what is being said. Critical listening is a much more active behaviour than informational listening and usually involves some sort of problem solving or decision making. Critical listening is akin to critical reading; both involve analysis of the information being received and alignment with what we already know or believe. Whereas informational listening may be mostly concerned with receiving facts and/or new information – critical listening is about analysing opinions and making a judgement. When the word 'critical' is used to describe listening, reading or thinking it does not necessarily mean that you are claiming that the information you are listening to is somehow faulty or flawed. Rather, critical listening means engaging in what you are listening to by asking yourself questions such as, 'what is the speaker trying to say?' or 'what is the main argument being presented?', 'how does what I'm hearing differ from my beliefs, knowledge or opinion?' Critical listening is, therefore, very important to the true learning of a leader. Most day-to-day decisions that we make are based on some form of 'critical' analysis, whether it be critical listening, reading or thinking. Our opinions, values and beliefs are based on our ability to process information and formulate our own feelings about the world around us, as well as weigh up the pros and cons to make an informed decision.

The LOS podcast lets me have interesting conversations with leaders around the world, and I have been fortunate to talk with Walter Revell, who is the chairman of the board in three organisations trading in the NASDAQ. He is also the emeritus chairman of Norwegian Cruise Line Holdings (the third largest cruise lines holding), Norwegian Cruise Line, Regent Seven Seas Cruises and Oceania Cruises. This is what he told me:

"The first 20 years of your career you learn from others, followed by 20 years where you lead others and the next 20 years you listen to others."

It is therefore important, when listening critically, to be open-minded and not be biased by stereotypes or preconceived ideas. By doing this, you will become a better listener and broaden your knowledge and perception of other people and your relationships with them. As a leader, this is key to your success.

11. "EMPATHIC LISTENING, ALEXA & SIRI DEVICES ARE FAR FROM UNDERSTANDING!!"

Empathic listening involves attempting to understand the feelings and emotions of the speaker – to put yourself into their shoes and share their thoughts. You will often come across this with good managers and you may well recall them as such. This is a skill which will make you or break you as a leader. Even though we have artificial intelligence like Siri, and Alexa, these devices are very far from understanding emotional communication.

Empathy is a way of deeply connecting with another person, and therapeutic or empathic listening can be particularly challenging. Empathy is not the same as sympathy, it involves more than being compassionate or feeling sorry for somebody else – it involves a deeper connection – a realisation and understanding of another person's point of view.

Counsellors, therapists and some other professionals use therapeutic or empathic listening to understand and ultimately help their clients. This type of listening does not involve making judgements or offering advice, but gently encouraging the speaker to explain and elaborate on their feelings and emotions. Skills, such as clarification and reflection, are often used to help avoid misunderstandings.

We are all capable of empathic listening and may practise it with friends, family and colleagues. Showing empathy is a desirable trait in many interpersonal relationships – you may well feel more comfortable talking about your own feelings and emotions with a particular person. They are likely to be better at listening empathetically to you than others. This is often based on similar perspectives, experiences, beliefs and values – a good friend, your spouse, a parent or sibling, for example.

Here is a model I have developed called the C.R.A.M.B.E.R which is listed below in my 7 tips to improve your listening skills:

C – Concentrate on the speaker – in a very broad sense. Not only does this refer to the physical act of body language, but also to picking up on non-verbal and other signals; tone of voice, body language and facial expressions, often giving life to the message.

R – Respond quickly once the message has been 'heard' to reaffirm your understanding. Factors like language and accent may affect your understanding.

A – Ask questions occasionally to clarify meaning and allow the speaker an opportunity to rephrase or underline a point.

M – Make notes on the key points. Even if you do not refer to them, they will help to focus your mind. Importantly here, the listener also needs to be aware of, and avoid any preconceptions or biases that they hold that may affect how the message is interpreted.

B – Be alert to the nuances of what the speaker is saying.

E – Evaluating requires that you keep an open mind on the messages that you are receiving and don't jump to conclusions about what is being said. Evaluate all the information and only then start to formulate a response.

R – Responding. Finally, your response should be well-measured and demonstrate that you have understood what was communicated. It may be necessary to use techniques such as clarifying and reflecting as part of your response.

Leavers to Leaders Listen to Others

Network Effectively

In the early days of my business life, I used to attend a lot of networking events. I have to say some of them were useful while others were a complete waste of my time. Time is your biggest asset – you can get more money but not more time. So, as a leaver, networking becomes very important and if you have a time limit then you need to understand the value of social networking. There are a lot of social platforms available. I personally don't use all of them, but the three main ones are Facebook, LinkedIn and Twitter. You can also use Instagram and link it to Facebook. You may argue why you should network online and offline, but I believe you need both. Since the world has become more digital, you can reach out to almost anyone in the world via those social media.

As a leader, you need to know how to manage this new domain in your life effectively. We will explore this in more detail in Chapter 6: Leading Oneself.

I think it is important to know about yourself first before you go out to network. Networking is an ongoing and continuous process. You network during work when you communicate with others, you network at events and you network online. Each time I have a meeting with someone I haven't met, I always do my research and look at their social profile before meeting them. So make sure your own details are up to date, relevant and professional. You can manage your profile as you wish, but remember that people are always likely to look you up.

Let's first examine what type of networker you are.

IMA digital[8] is an online colour-coded test created by James Knight to give you an idea of what type of networker you are online. High Green means: time disciplined, logical, respectful, structured, well organised and precise. High Blue means being pleasant, non-assertive, selfless, supportive and sincere. High Red means: practical, assertive, to the point, and goal-oriented. High Yellow means: flexible, positive, generous, quick and supportive of ideas. This test will give you an idea of your online behaviour. You can also identify this colour for the people you interact with as well.

The next important aspect of your networking is working to understand the people around you better. As I was doing research in this area, I remembered reading Dale Carnegie's book, 'How to Win Friends and Influence People'. The content in this book changed my life. One of its key messages is to connect with people genuinely. The book was published in 1936, a time where no social media environment existed and the author talks about a gang leader who was arrested for killing several people. When questioned, he revealed that he was just looking for people to like him as he was. My take on all this is that if you are in the business of people and you are looking to influence others as leader, you must be interested in people. I

---

[8] http://ima-digital.com

am lucky to be bicultural in my upbringing and a citizen of the world. I like the way the British handle things, never wanting to offend you even if they are not totally supportive towards an idea or concept. The French, on the other hand, can be very dogmatic in their opinions which can sometimes be seen as aggressive. Interestingly, when you are genuinely interested in people, they also become genuinely interested in you. I remember in 2015 during a visit to one of the largest American aircraft carriers to Portsmouth, I was assigned to work with the Commanding Officer of *USS Theodore Roosevelt,* CVN 71 Captain Daniel Grieco.

Now, a man of his calibre is pretty difficult to get hold of, but working with him was another enjoyable experience. As the CO of *USS Theodore Roosevelt,* he had the responsibility of 5,000 troops onboard and I remember asking him how he managed all of them. His reply was: 'When I do my daily walk on the bridge, I meet new people daily. The team rotates every 90 days with a new team and it is almost impossible to know each of my officers and team individually. However, my role as their CO is for them to know that I will bring them back home to their family regardless of the situation.'

This is a pretty strong statement and I am sure if you were on this huge aircraft carrier, you would feel pretty safe and comfortable. Daniel is now a veteran and we have stayed connected. The lesson of this story is to be genuinely interested in people. He was a CO of CVN71, I was just there to work with him during his visit in the UK, but it was my genuine interest in him, not his rank, which made it possible to have him in my network. As you decide to become a leader in your field, be aware of your surroundings and be interested in people regardless of their level in the company.

People will also remember how you made them feel. People can always forget your mistakes but they will never forget the emotions you left them with.

Here are 7 steps to help you network effectively:

1. Take the IMA test at www.ima-digital.com
2. Become more aware of your social environment.
3. Become aware of your online network.
4. Connect with people genuinely.
5. Remember that your first impression still counts, even more with an online profile.
6. Be genuinely interested in people; we are all humans.
7. Always leave people better than you find them. People always remember how you made them feel.

Leavers to Leaders Listen to Others

Check Your Ego

Everyone has an ego. Ego drives the most successful people in life: in the military, in the workplace and in business. Ego makes you want to win an argument, a conversation, or make a point. But ego also clouds your judgement and prevents you from seeing the world as it is. Ego can become destructive to your personal self and your career. When personal agendas become more important than the workplace and its success, the workplace suffers, and failure is guaranteed. Many times the main issues arising in a team can be attributed to a problem of ego. Ego clouds and disrupts everything, it will affect your vision and the ability to accept constructive criticism: Nine out of ten times, the most difficult ego to deal with is your own.

During his time in The White House, President Theodore Roosevelt admitted he was right 75 percent of the time. If this was the highest percentage someone of his position could get, what about you and me? If you can be right even 55 percent of the time, then you would be making some great progress against the odds. If this is the case, then why should we tell others when *they* are wrong?

You will never get to the next level if you do not keep your ego in check. Sometimes it is not about win-lose, it is about collaboration, it is about win-win. As you prepare yourself on this journey to leadership, you need to master your ego, because as we will see in Chapter 6, it plays a vital part as you move up the ladder. In the military, there is a constant shift of ego. For example, the Paras think they are the most aggressive in battles, the Gurkhas think they are the most agile in the front line, and the Royal Marines think they are the best in engaging the enemy. However put those three elite teams together and you have a hell of a team able to do some heavy damage in the enemy camp.

I have, several times in my military career, been involved in joint operations by all three services in the British Armed forces, which are: British Army, Royal Marines/ Royal Navy and the Royal Air Force – especially at the beginning of my career and in 2001, leading up to the war on Iraq and Afghanistan. As a young movement controller, we had helicopters flying into the Sea Mounting Centre from the Army Air Corps, power boats arriving from the port side and tanks arriving by low loader from the army, and vehicles from the RAF. It was one of the most coordinated mounting operations I have come across so far in my life and I was right in the centre of it.

Everyone had their ego in check. Earlier that week the Ministry of Defence had hired 50 roll-on roll-off ships from Turkey to facilitate this deployment in getting into Karachi in Pakistan. We already had a team flying to Karachi and setting up the receiving port. In a state of war, I witnessed some of the best win-win operations. No one cared about who was what or from which service, especially when you are in combat uniform. As a matter of fact, this experience has had such an impact on my life that, a few years later I founded TriExForces with the same principle of a collaborative approach.

To be a leader and keep growing, you need to surround yourself with people who aren't afraid to tell you the uncomfortable truths in a polite way, and if you truly respect someone with power over you, you'll do the same.

Chris is on a mission to cure obesity. During his upbringing, he had over four jobs a day. By the time he was 16, he joined the British army, and a few years later he went on to become an Airborne. He has done very well in his career and we will be hearing from him later in this book. What I admire about Chris is that he has worked with huge egos in his career, and has been willing to take on his own ego as well, while taking his wealth to the next level. Understanding how to cultivate people around you who are not afraid to tell you the truth is a key component, and to do that, you need to start by checking your own ego. Jon Gordon, author of 'The Root of Success', stresses that a leader should "focus on the root not the fruit." You are the root of your workplace.

You want to be a leader? Get better outcomes? Be recognised by others? Then think of yourself as the root of your organisation and soon enough you will be known for it.

During my LOS podcast talk with Paul Bennett, Director of Enterprise Southampton Business School, University of Southampton. I found out how he was head-hunted into a role at Henley School of Business back when he was sailing round the world in his 67 ft sailing boat delivering training for leaders. Someone recognised him as the root and saw his leadership abilities.

So here are 7 tips to help you manage and check your ego:

1. Always be quick to admit when you are wrong.
2. No one can be 100% correct, so expect to be wrong.
3. Encourage others to correct you positively.
4. Be comfortable being corrected by others, even if they might be your junior.
5. Always think win-win.
6. Do a self-appraisal on yourself.
7. See yourself as the root not the fruit.

Leavers to Leaders Listen to Others

Use Their Mindpower

During a conference in 2017 by Theo Paphitis, the former BBC Dragons' Den panellist and the Chancellor of Solent University, he talked about using other people's ideas. In the 21st century, where everything has already been invented and created, there is not much you can do to reinvent the wheel. However, there are still a lot of ideas and different ways to communicate. For example, most of the disruption we are going to experience with technology such as Uber or Airbnb or Just Eat are just a better way to communicate between the product and the end user. They are not reinventing the taxi trade, or the hospitality industry, nor the way we eat. Thanks to Amazon who led this new wave of click-on-demand services. If you look at the iPad, the idea existed many years before Steve Jobs. It so happens that Alan Kay wrote a paper entitled, "A Personal Computer for Children of All Ages," you get the impression that the author had a clear vision of a device like the iPad. Remember, this was 38 years ago in a time when the phrase "personal computer" did not exist, when there was no Microsoft, and computers were not common. I'll spare you the details of the paper and you can read the text or download the PDF of the article to learn about a part of computer history you don't hear about that often.[9]

Clearly, if big corporations and business leaders are talking

---

[9] https://www.mprove.de/diplom/gui/kay72.html

about using other people's brains, there must be a value in doing so. We should consider the vast amount of experience and privilege we can get from baby boomers who have lived through not just the 2008 recession, but also the great recessions of the 70s, 80s and 90s. Currently we have about ten thousand baby boomers retiring daily, and if you can tap into their knowledge, the benefit can be huge.

Now, don't take this the wrong way: there is *using* other people's ideas and *stealing* their ideas, which is completely wrong and unethical. But sometimes the best of knowledge can come from the least expected of people as well. Back in the day, I remember meeting with someone in London who suggested that the care industry is a promising industry where many have actually made their success. The idea stayed with me for almost four years, until in 2007 my wife and I opened our first care home looking after people with learning disabilities. So sometimes, people can implant an idea or thought into your brain, and it is up to you how you let this idea grow. It was surely very difficult for myself and my wife to think that far, after all we didn't even have a home, as we were tenants living in military married quarters. She worked hard as a carer, while I was busy with unsociable hours in the military due to 9/11. But the idea grew slowly, and in June 2004 we bought our first house which gave way to our first small residential care home.

Your journey as a leaver to leader depends on a lot of factors but, most importantly, it depends on you. You need to decide what ideas you are listening to, and you need to decide which thoughts you will let grow.

So leadership success is in your hand. You will find yourself surrounded by two types of people: those who have your best interests at heart and those who pretend they do. You need to decide which ones will influence you.

Environment influences output. When you were a toddler, you had a limited ability to make independent decisions, like when to cross the road, for instance. Back then, your parents used clear words to tell you how to behave, such as, "You should never cross the street alone". But now you're old enough to cross safely by yourself and to make your own decisions, like being around the right people – the kind that can guide you through a difficult crossroad.

12 CROSSROADS IN LIFE, BEING AROUND THE RIGHT PEOPLE THAT CAN GUIDE YOU IN MAKING YOUR OWN DECISIONS!!

This part of the book is not about excuses, blame, or impossible dreams. It is about enabling you to make the most of what you have, how to learn, and know who you are surrounded by, so you can make the best decisions on how you plan your transition. It is about preparing yourself to make the jump, based on both the facts and how you have developed yourself over the years.

Do you feel as though some of what life has to offer is behind you? Who or what are you blaming for keeping you from your goals? Why have you not been able to live the life you want? Is it money? Is it your spouse? Your children? Your current job? It is "them"?

We will look at the power of imagination later in Chapter 5 as you lead yourself. This is not just about achieving success, but also about having a purpose and creating significance. This in turn will help you see that a job is not just about earning a living, but also about considering how many hours a day you spend on it. Your current job is a vehicle for pursuing your passion. I often see a lot of veterans moving from one job to another, and I can totally relate to this experience, as until you find your true passion, you will not be totally happy in your current job. Service personnel may join the military for many reasons but in the end they stay in because of their mates. The relationships and bonds between service personnel last for a lifetime and sometimes this is the problem when transitioning.

As a leaver, you need to embrace change. Change is happening and you are already surrounded by people who have the knowledge and skills you need. If you don't, then you may have to change your environment.

Here are 7 steps for you to become more aware of other people's mindset:

1. Be aware of your entourage.
2. Surround yourself with people who can stretch your thinking.
3. Remember that environment influences output.
4. Be willing to consider other people's ideas.
5. Spend time finding your passion.
6. Ask those close to you what they think moves you.
7. Listen to those close to you – you will be surprised how much they know about you already.

CHAPTER 4

Leavers To Leaders Learn From Others

Be Genuine

I had the opportunity to meet with the former owner of The Cloud Hotel in Lyndhurst, Hampshire, Avril Owton. We had a lovely conversation as she shared with me her personal story as a former Tiller girl and how she made her journey to become a business leader, being awarded an MBE for her work with helping women around the world. While she was signing a copy of her book for me, she said, 'You must have a story, go tell the world about it.' At that time, we had just launched our training division at TriExForces and the idea didn't resonate with me, but she planted a seed which after a few years started to grow.

Learning from others is such an important part of your journey as a leaver to a leader. You see, we are lucky to be surrounded by those who have been there before us, the baby boomers and about 10,000 of them are going into retirement every day. They have worked hard, paid their dues and they can be your best teachers. I have such fun when I talk with them during the LOS Podcast, learn about their victories and also pitfalls just so I can learn from their experiences.

In the previous chapter, we talked about networking for collaboration. We have identified the different types of people and how to notice them and how to learn from them. What psychologists call the intelligence quotient (IQ) is just an attempt to quantify human intelligence. The problem with this is that intelligence is hard to pin down and define. It is difficult to measure IQ with happiness, health, and wealth. There is even some evidence that people with high IQs tend to befriend less people and have less friendships, because they have trouble making friends with people they consider less intelligent than themselves. On the other hand, people tend to be less comfortable around someone who seems to be too smart for their own good. There are exceptions, like Bill Gates, founder of Microsoft, and Warren Buffett – both exceptionally brilliant leaders with high IQs. But they are the minority. Your Connectivity Quotient on the other side is measured by your ability to have many friends and large professional and social networks, which definitely will make you happier, healthier and of course a better person. If close relationships and friendships can make such a difference in your health and happiness, imagine what those relationships and friendships can help you achieve in your career as a leader.

Look back at the major developments – the invention of the

telegraph in the 1830s, the telephone in 1876, radio in 1895, and television in 1927 – and now, the growing rates of social networking are all making it easier for us to connect. Understand that, as humans, we need to cultivate connections. As a leader, one of your main roles is to serve others. This is your business, even if you are a bus driver, coffee shop owner or a CEO.

Change your mindset and everything else around you will change.

After I enlisted in the British Armed Forces, I was always looking for ways to do more, not just so that I got promoted but so that I could be different. I was different and unique with my bicultural status. Up to this day, when I meet a new person, I make sure they see my Mauritius side. This normally ends up with 'what are you doing here' or 'I always wanted to go there' or 'it is on my bucket list'. To this, I now reply, "Why not join one of our leadership summits which takes place in Mauritius?"

A good analogy is when you hire a car. Do you take it for a car wash before you return it? Of course not. It is not your car, so you don't have to care about it. It doesn't belong to you!

I am not saying this is the way we should be, but that this is the way we are. We tend to not pay attention to things that do not belong to us. Treat your workplace with respect as a place of belonging, as the people around you are your best resource from which to learn. I understand that this does not come naturally for everyone. Some people find cheerfulness and camaraderie is not their strength. Plenty of people don't see themselves as a people person. They may have issues with shyness, social anxiety, or self-confidence, and this can make it hard to talk with new people. In England, it is actually one of the easier things to do, since we all like to talk about the weather which can be so unpredictable: I have found that weather talk is one of the best ways to engage in the UK.

In 2010, I was on my way back from Mauritius via Dubai. Unfortunately, due to the volcanic eruption in Norway and the ash cloud created, there was a no-fly zone into UK airspace. So I was stuck for seven days in Dubai. I met with another traveller from Jordan and we decided to explore Dubai together. By chance he spoke a little bit of Arabic. He took me to some of the best parts of Dubai and for the very first time I visited a mosque. It was huge and very nicely decorated with marble. By the time he left, I felt like I knew Dubai like the back of my hand. On another occasion during the same trip, myself and a British couple from Bristol were in the same line trying to get a flight to the UK. We could get a flight to Manchester, but not London. We all looked at each other and Jane, Thomas and I quickly decided that was a better option than waiting another few days. We agreed to share a car hire from Manchester. I did most of the driving since I had to carry on driving to Southampton after dropping them in Bristol. All of these people were complete strangers and I learned a lot from all of them. One was a businessman, while Jane and Thomas were two university professors with different IQ. All three were genuine, and people will sense this.

You can learn from others' wisdom and also from others' mistakes and this is what we are covering in the next chapter.

Here are my 7 action steps for you to be genuine:

1. Be comfortable with yourself.
2. If you find it hard to be around people, learn how to change.
3. You must accept the journey. It is a journey.
4. Be wary of online friends. The Internet has been revolutionary in connecting us online. Face to face is the real interaction – these are people you can pick up the phone and talk to.
5. Learn to make your face reveal the sincere warmth and interest that turns strangers into friends. Practise in front of a mirror and smile. No one wants to talk with a bored-looking person.
6. Try to look animated when you speak. People will converse with you in a far more focused fashion.
7. Give people your full attention. Don't just act interested – be interested.

Leavers To Leaders Learn From Others

Learn from Their Mistakes

One of the main mistakes I made with my career in the British Armed Forces was leaving without having a full pension in place. These days, a full pension at the age of 42 is very welcome, especially if you successfully reinvent yourself by applying the steps in this book. But guess what. I don't think there would be any book, nor would there be any better experiences, without my transition. The ability to learn from others' mistakes is even more important than their successes. I absolutely enjoy sharing my mistakes so others can learn. Keep in mind that for people to share their deepest regrets and mistakes there has to be a circle of trust.

Steven R. Covey, author of 'The 7 Habits of Highly Successful People', once said that: people don't trust you because they don't know you and when they get to know you they don't trust you.

Trust is at the core of every relationship, personal or professional. I had the honour to have people who shared their mistakes with me in the past and some of those are like red flashing lights to me even to this day. In one particular talk with a former CEO, he said he wished to have taken more risks and ignored fear of failure.

> *If you can control your own thoughts, you won't have to be concerned about others' actions.*

When you respect others, they can teach you and share with you some of their most valuable lessons in life, whether personal or professional. Their good and not-so-good stories can change your life forever.

There is a story about two children in Africa who were playing with rocks when some explorers approached them and offered them candy in exchange for the rocks. The children gladly traded, not knowing that they had a fortune in their hands. This is a sad story of how sometimes our talents are wasted at work when they are overlooked and undervalued; we trade them in for a job that may never recognise our full potential.

13 "NEVER OVERLOOK AN OPPORTUNITY... RECOGNISE YOUR FULL POTENTIAL!"

Many of us are the same. You are surrounded by people with talents and skills, but also who have made many mistakes, which you can learn from as you transition as a leader. As a leader, I am more interested to know about the mistakes of others than the successes, and this has always been my attitude to learning.

However, be aware that the negativity other people place on you can kill your positive energy. A few years ago, avoiding negative energy was much easier, as you simply withdrew yourself from the midst of negative people. I have not come across any news since 2008 that is good news. These types of stories are easily accessible on your phone: your phone is your TV and it is in your hand 24/7. This means that news – and mostly bad news – is everywhere and you cannot escape it, especially if you have Facebook, Twitter or any social media.

Have you come across someone whose behaviour changed after browsing their phone and seeing something, whether good or bad? Bad news from the media is not for you to learn from, but will suck your positive vibes. Instead, make appointments with people who you trust and seek to learn from their mistakes. You will make more progress by listening to their mistakes and advice than trying to reinvent the wheel to finding out what is working and what is not working.

My dream is to do for others what my mentors did for me.

Your role is to leave a legacy for the next generation and learn from the legacy left by the past generations. Young people must be told that they, as individuals, are more important than what they wear, what phone they use or what they drive. When you get in the habit of learning from others' mistakes, you will also be able to understand teenagers better, your colleagues better, and how to impact their lives. You may have heard the saying: the apple never falls far from the tree. I've been reminded of this a few times by my wife. My eldest daughter can sleep from 9pm to 11am the next day, and sometimes I get irritated by the time she wakes up. Well, of course, this happens only at the weekend.

Then, I was reminded how I also like sleeping and how one day I missed my interview to join the Mauritius police force due to this. This was a mistake which could have taken a very different toll on my life. As it turns out, both my mum and my dad were against the idea of me joining the police.

Here are 7 ways to learn from others' mistakes:

1. For you to learn from others' mistakes, be careful in your approach and be genuinely interested in the person.
2. Always show respect to others, regardless of age, race or gender.
3. Ask for help.
4. Avoid hanging around negative people, they will only bring you down and then walk over you.
5. Remember there are two reasons people won't trust you: they don't know you, or they feel they cannot trust you.
6. Be a motivator for others. No one wants to hang out for coffee with someone who is going to suck the life out of them.
7. Be genuine about your intentions with others; let them know what you are hoping to learn from them.

Leavers to Leaders Learn From Others

Dream Spirit

One of my rocks in life is my mother. Since I was a little boy, she has always had my best interests in mind. Sometimes I can't see clearly, like in 2001. It had only been two years since my dad passed away, and I didn't have all the funding I needed after paying for my flight and education fees to do my studies in London. I had taken a two-year leave without pay from Mauritius Freeport Authority, fairly granted to me by the then CEO, Gerard Sanspeur. There was going to be no income for me and, as the eldest son in my family, I was responsible for my mother and my little sister. These are my African values. Since my dad had completed his long and good service in the police force for 29 years, my mother would get his pension and a lump sum. Me asking her to pay for my flight was more than just a gamble. She did it, because she believed in my dream spirit, always has, and as Abraham Lincoln said: "All that I am and all I ever hope to be, I owe to my mother."

In your life, you need to be surrounded by people who dream like you or whose dreams are bigger than yours. There is a good story of a man called Joseph who had ten older brothers. Joseph was a dreamer and would share his dream with his father and his brothers. Unfortunately not all of them agreed with his dream and vision and decided to hinder him. He was put into a pit, then sold as a slave. But then, one day, he showed up as the Vizier of Egypt, the second most powerful man next to the Pharaoh. There is a lot more detail to this story and you will find it in the Bible in the Book of Genesis.

It is important to realise that in life you will encounter the good, the bad and the jealous on your journey, the same as Joseph did with his own 10 brothers. These characters are likely to always be in your life, and you may not always be able to identify them, but they will be there. You will always encounter detractors in your personal life and your profession. Hence why you need to be careful with whom you share your dream and vision. People sometimes don't mean to stop you, it is the fear that they cannot comprehend or perhaps they don't have the same vision for their own life, and you can learn from that. Learn to preserve your dream spirit.

Now that we have got the bad out of the way, let's focus on the good.

Sometimes, when you pursue your goal, your vision or your dream, it can be difficult to make a mental leap from where you are to where you want to be. Seizing the opportunity that lies ahead demands an expanded consciousness. Sometimes it may feel like too much of a stretch to say, "I can do it," and you may want to abandon the journey. When these thoughts and behaviours occur in your mind, you need to establish a place to go mentally to get your bearings and to get your focus. We will explore that in Chapter 5 on Leading Oneself.

In life, you must consciously engage yourself with others and share their dreams. When you serve others and help them to get to where they want to be, you will also develop a mentality to work on yourself harder. If you want an easy life, things will become hard. If you work hard, life becomes easier. Aristotle said:

> *"To be conscious of what you are perceiving or thinking is to be conscious of your own existence."*

A lot of people believe they are doing all they can for their lives. You need to see yourself as being vital in order to contribute to yourself, others and your organisation. If you can be replaced, then you are simply functional. The power to become a leader is within you. I have come across many who live their life based on their past experiences and limited awareness. It is a cruise to nowhere. Their talents and gifts will never be put to use. It is very sad.

You need to learn, learn, learn and sometimes you need to abandon the old tools and take on new ones. This is especially true in business where many things can be automated and become technology driven. There are enough examples already of firms and industries which have changed – just look around and you can learn a lot about the future of work.

When you grow your consciousness, you will start to learn more from others and you will see a mindset shift in yourself. Like Joseph, you will want to share it with others. You will face obstacles, some will take you down, but it is your ability to get up and keep pushing

that will make the difference. This book is titled 'Leaver to Leader' but the process is actually about YOU and about you unfolding your future. Instead of being in your own way, be on your way.

Here are the 7 action steps to learn about your dreams. (There are no right or wrong answers):

1. Get to know what others think about you – remember the good, the bad and the jealous.
2. Find out what motivates you – family, kids, better future, happy life, helping others. This list is inexhaustible.
3. It is your purpose to provide for your family and give your family the best quality of life possible. Your "free" time should be spent with your family, and for your family.
4. Is your purpose on earth to do as much good for as many people as possible during your lifetime?
5. Lead a more adventurous life, meet different people, eat something new, get comfortable with change.
6. Be like Joseph. Have a dream about your life, what would you do, where you would go, who would you help.
7. Remember the Law of Attraction. If you want a blue Ford Galaxy, you will begin to see more and more of them on the road, because your brain is set to look for them.

One final point before moving into the 3 LOS of Leadership. Use the above as a scale with your typical self-centred person on one end and imagine someone like Mother Teresa or Gandhi on the other end. Where do you see yourself? Would you like to move? If you have a significant other in your life, will they support you? If they don't, you will need to realign your dream spirit with them.

The above exercise is very important in finding your life purpose. You must be at peace with yourself and your desire from life to have the confidence, and enjoy the journey reaching for your goals.

CHAPTER 5

Leavers to Leaders Lead Oneself

Become Entrepreneurial

The world is changing and so must you. We are now in a digital revolution where technology is replacing humans. It has now become easier to check out at Sainsburys and easier to get a cab in under five minutes than speaking with a human. You may still remember the age of Blockbuster, where you could happily walk into a shop, look around for a DVD, get a popcorn, get everyone around to watch the film, and all that in under one hour! Now you can watch any film of your liking with a click or touch of your remote. Ten years ago, the world was in a different place. Click & Collect – or kerbside pick-up if you are in the US – appeared for if you don't even want to get out of your car! Amazon has already announced it is bringing Prime Now pickup to whole foods and groceries. Even Nike has its own version of kerbside pickup with it latest high-tech store in Los Angeles, which works with a text messaging service called Swoosh Text.

I often talk with people who are transitioning from the military, from all ranks and ages. After much observation, I believe most people build a career until the ages of 40 to 45, then they coast. Why, I do not know, whether they get comfortable, secure, or simply happy with the status quo. Those leaving the military are mostly in their mid-40s and, having completed one career, are now in a position to step into a new one.

15.
"A WALK AFTER A HARD DAY'S WORK ONCE YOU'VE GOTTEN HOME, IS EASILY ACHIEVABLE AND INOFFENSIVELY REWARDING!"

Make no mistake, there is a glass ceiling in many organisations and industries. Acknowledge that, but then it's up to you to work to achieve your goals. Never assume you can't get to a certain level just because of your gender or race. Go into every situation thinking you can succeed – just have your eyes open. If you do run into a glass ceiling, deal with it as best as you can. Most people will struggle to do so. Why? Because the scariest thing is that we are now facing a digital world.

Consultancy firm, Deloitte, conducted a study of the future of London in the face of technology. The study, called Agiletown, looked at a few major industries including: transport, education, skills, infrastructure, retail work and place. This study reveals that some jobs are more at risk than others. For example, the report says that the jobs more at risk are in administrative support, sales, construction and manufacturing. The jobs least affected by automation are in skilled management, such as financial services, art and media, healthcare, legal services, community services and education.[10] The report goes on to say that people in London earning around £30 000 are more likely to be replaced by automation than those earning £100 000. This means almost 35% of UK jobs are at risk and can be replaced by computers.

In the United States, according to an Oxford University study, 47% of the total workforce is at risk due to computerisation, and many jobs can be replaced by technology or automation[11].

---

[10] https://www2.deloitte.com/content/dam/Deloitte/uk/Documents/uk-futures/london-futures-agiletown.pdf
[11] https://www.oxfordmartin.ox.ac.uk/downloads/academic/The_Future_of_Employment.pdf

They are referring mostly to manual or low-skilled work requiring physical labour. The study shows that as many as 140 million full-time workers could be replaced by advanced algorithms.

The World Economic Forum in its report reveals that by 2022, around 54% of the workforce will need to reinvent themselves or invest in reskilling.

We have already seen technology replacing humans even in the world of fashion, which is generally thought to be a human-driven environment – such as a catwalk using VR technology in 2016 in London. This wasn't so much about capturing and replicating an experience – more about transporting users by creating one layered over the real world. Attendees to emerging London designer Martine Jarlgaard's show, wore Microsoft HoloLens headsets to see the full spring/summer 2017 collection coming to life in the form of holograms in front of them, so everyone could explore the collection from all angles.[12] This provided fans with a fully-immersive version of a classically-flat live stream experience – enabling them to feel as though they were sitting in the front row.

If you are to be a leader in the workplace, you cannot ignore such research. It's almost guaranteed that you won't be in your current job for the remainder of your working life. No matter how hard you work, how many hours you work a week, how well you get on with your boss, how many fantastic ideas and

---

[12] https://www.theguardian.com/media-network/2016/sep/23/tech-fashion-week-burberry-tommy-hilfiger-virtual-reality

projects you have launched, how much revenue you bring into the company, your days as an employee in any particular industry are numbered. My dad worked in one job for thirty-one years until he passed away at the age of forty-nine. Statistics used to say that you would change your job at least seven times in your lifetime. New research is suggesting that by the time you are thirty, you will have had seven careers. Whether you work for a global company, SME, or small business, your ability to succeed depends on how you position yourself as a leader.

You will get paid by the amount of value you add to the workplace.

Your current job is also the best place to gain credibility while getting paid. It is the perfect place to figure out where you want to go and develop new skills that might help you succeed in your dream occupation, whatever that might be. As an entrepreneurial leader, you need to see your current employer not just as your client but also as your business. Work effectively and just plain hard for your business. As an entrepreneurial leader, you also need to be constantly looking for the next dream contract. Eventually, you will become headhunted for the next big job.

During my research for this book, I interviewed Hannah, 35 years old and working in the care industry. She used to help us when we had our small care business right after I left the military. During the interview, she was very keen to let me know that she is now a team leader and has four teams working for her. As we slowly switched the conversation on to her future aspiration and goals, she soon realised that some of her skills can also be used in the hospitality industry. Although she has lots of qualifications in the care industry, she would be better off if she had some leadership qualifications which would leverage her skills across any industry.

As we move into the digital world, according to the World Economic Forum, by 2020 5.1 million jobs will be disrupted and lost due to the technology trend around the world, and it is already happening[13]. We can now walk into Sainsbury's and pick our food and, pay at an automated checkout without having to have any human interaction. I have the same experience when I book my flight, print my tickets, walk into the terminal, check my bags, go through a security scanner and board my plane. It is already happening and we don't need to wait for advanced robots to come around, we can see or imagine automation.

So how do you make the most of this development. How do you become a leader in your field or any field of your choice? This is where the power to reinvent yourself comes in.

Now, being born on a tropical island surrounded by ocean, one thing I am a great fan of are lobsters, and perhaps the lobster analogy is the best one to help you understand how to reinvent yourself. Lobsters are part of the crustacean family. They have a hard exoskeleton shell that protects them, while also containing them. A lobster de-shells 20 to 30 times in its life, and each time the de-shelling takes place, the lobster is exposed. It is at risk of

---

[13] http://www3.weforum.org/docs/WEF_Future_of_Jobs.pdf

being eaten and picked at by all the other sea creatures. The formation of a new shell takes about 10 days. In the life of a lobster, this is a hell of a time, and during that time the lobster is out of its comfort zone. The lobster has to be comfortable being uncomfortable in order to grow and be this majestic creature. Each time it leaves the old shell behind, the flesh is exposed to other prowlers of the sea. But it is also very interesting, as any part of its limbs which are missing, including its eyes and antennae, are regenerated. In order to be a leader beyond 2020, you need to reinvent yourself all the time, taking more risk and stepping out of your comfort zone. Of course, a lot of people will pick at you, and you also need to be comfortable with that.

So, be a lobster and take on new challenges and learn new skills. Be comfortable to be uncomfortable.

In the next chapters we will cover the 5 main parts of leading oneself through an uncomfortable journey and becoming comfortable with change.

Here are my 7 action steps to becoming more entrepreneurial:

1. Stop seeing yourself as an employee. See yourself as an entrepreneurial leader, no matter what the job.
2. Become comfortable with challenging the status quo.
3. Dream big about your ideal lifestyle: the one you have will also change.
4. Take on more responsibility at work.
5. Become a lobster – de-shell and embrace new things.
6. Read more about businesses and entrepreneurs, as they challenge the world.
7. Take daily action to review the value you contribute to the workplace.

Leavers to Leaders: Leading Oneself

Emotional and Spiritual Well-Being

In the next chapter, we will cover the five main parts of leading oneself through an uncomfortable journey and becoming comfortable with it.

Before we begin, stop worrying and start the process of reinventing yourself. If an average guy like me can do it, so can you – and the sooner you start, the better you can readjust and realign.

So relax, rejoice, refocus, and let's re-energise because this is your time to shine.

Since I have been out of the military, there are three things that have always stayed with me:

The motto for the Royal Air Force is Per Ardua ad Astra: "Through Adversity to the Stars." (Latin)

For the Royal Navy it is: "Si vis pacem, para bellum" (Latin); "If you wish for peace, prepare for war."

For the British Army it is: "Be the best."

When I examine each of these mottos, I realise how each is significant in a leader's life. Each of the above were written to set a standard and motivate the personnel. What does it takes to 'be the best', 'through adversity to the stars' and 'if you wish for peace prepare for war'. Those mottos have been around for years but are undervalued in their meaning.

In stepping out of your comfort zone, one of the key elements to keep in mind is your emotional being. This plays a crucial part in your day-to-day life. It's one thing to sense the world around you, and it's another to truly experience it. There is a clear distinction between the outside world and you... until emotions come into the mix.

When we experience emotions in response to things that happen outside of ourselves, we're forming a connection to those things and to the world outside of our skin. Emotional well-being is crucial to living a life of wholeness, balance, and contentment. Simply put, emotional well-being is made up of many things, including the ability to get up when life knocks you down. Rather than living a problem-free life (quite impossible if you're a human being), emotional well-being means that one can bounce back from setbacks and thrive despite problems.

When it comes to drive, diligence, focus and dedication, we need to believe that we are personally invested in order to achieve maximum effort. Emotions are that investment. One of the greatest skills a person functioning in our world can have is empathy. Empathy allows us to put ourselves in another person's shoes, to see the world through their eyes, and feel the way that they feel. This is incredibly important, as empathising helps you understand how other people function – why they do the things that they do. It allows us to form personal connections with individuals. Unless we understand empathy, we will be forever alone. Even when we're surrounded by masses of people, we won't feel connected to them. Before you can connect with others, you need to be able to connect with yourself. You need to learn to deal with your emotions so they never get the better of you.

> "Learn to deal with your emotions so they never get the better of you."

People might perceive you as weak when they notice that you feel things more deeply than they do. But vulnerability and emotion are closely tied to passion, which is crucial to living a fulfilling life.

My passions have led me down some dark roads, but I emerged ironclad, with an insatiable thirst for greatness. One of my greatest times when I had to check in with my emotions was on the morning of November 29, 1999. We had taken my dad to the emergency room the previous night and he was very poorly, but that morning my mum was preparing some soup for him when the phone rang. It was 6am. I picked up the phone and the guy on the other end announced that my dad had passed away in the night, and we should collect him. He was very short and brief. I cannot see how he could have announced it any differently. I turned and my mum was there looking at me, holding a pot of soup, and I couldn't speak. She had supported my dad through his three months of sickness. Now, it was not a time to cry, as both my mum and my sister, who was 12 at the time, needed me. In Mauritius, funerals take place on the same day or within 24 hours. So lots of planning had to be done, informing friends and family, so the next 7 hours were very stressful. To be honest, I cannot remember all of it; so much happened within such a short time. There are times when emotions have to be kept in check, and this was one of those times. I refused to let my emotions get the better of me. I cried a lot in the following few days, on my own. My boss at the time, Desire Tsang Man Kin, was a good friend of my dad's and gave me a few weeks off. Two years later I made yet another hard decision to leave my mum and sister and fly to London so that I could support them better financially. I controlled my emotions, because when you control your emotions, you will be unstoppable.

> *"You need to make your emotions work for you, and you will be unstoppable."*

There is a difference between being an emotional mess and letting your emotions control you.

Weakness is allowing your emotions to take the wheel. The more emotions you experience – the more emotions you can better understand – the more you will learn about yourself and people in general.

But you need to be willing to learn. Don't let your emotions govern your life. Make them work for you.

Learn to take a step back, observe your feelings from a distance, and make better life decisions.

Your spiritual well-being is an important part of you; it is that feeling inside of you that keeps you at peace. Your spiritual being is that greater sense of power that makes us believe in human kind, of having greater purpose and life. Your spiritual being has a deeper connectivity with the Almighty. Your spirituality is your sense of purpose on earth. Life is a journey, and spirituality is the bright torch that guides you and illuminates your path. Some people may not believe at all in religion and that is also fine, but I am pretty sure they believe in something they don't understand and perhaps cannot even explain. This is spirituality in its simplest form. Sometimes we think life gets easier, but I think we just get stronger.

Here are my 7 steps to improving your emotional and spiritual well-being:

1. Identify personal strengths, building them and living from them.
2. Learn optimism; realistically see the positive in even bad situations.
3. Develop the courage to define, and then live your life.
4. Embrace resilience and the ability to learn from and bounce back from setbacks.
5. Become flexible when facing challenges.
6. Have a social network, even if it is small.
7. Make time for hobbies and leisure.

Leavers to Leaders: Leading Oneself

Mental Well-Being

I used to think I was unstoppable — that even if you put a knife through me, I would still be marching on. This may well be a typical mental ego from anyone who has been through the military. We are taught to be fearless, we are taught to react to danger, we are taught to kill. Now that I have got your attention, so keep reading.

About a year ago, I suddenly woke up one Sunday morning to feel the left side of my face a little bit numb. You know that feeling you get when you've had an injection from the dentist. I didn't take much notice until I realised I was losing my facial expression on the left side of my face. I spoke to my friend about it — now, Isaac has always been my go-to guy for medical issues. We went to A&E only to find out that I had 'Bell's Palsy' which is a neuro-malfunction of the lower part of the brain. As most will know, in neuro science, the brain is the most complex structure known to human kind. To make matters worse, about a week later, both parts of my face had gone numb, so now I had lost all my ability to talk, smile, blink and was also having difficulty swallowing. My wife was scared and so were my three daughters and my team as I waited for a week at Southampton Neurological Centre undergoing all sorts of brain tests and examinations. This time, it was confirmed: I had Bilateral Bell's Palsy, a brain malfunction that occurs to 1:5,000,000. I guess I was the chosen one.

So since then, I have been a bit of a curious guy on brain function and mental health. Coming from the military, I know of many peers from the military and blue light services who suffered from PTSD due to the high impact of the front line and this is becoming more of a common problem today. We talked about the importance of social well-being in previous chapters and its impact of our lives.

So, as I am discovering more about this important part of our lives, I have come to realise that our mental well-being is the most important of our being, and managing our mental health is as important as managing our physical health. But before we find out ways to manage our mental well-being, let's find out more on how the brain functions.

The brain is made of two key parts: the prefrontal cortex which is right behind your forehead (critical for decision making, focus, attention and your personality). The second key part is the temporal lobe located on the left and right side of the rear of the brain. Deep in the temporal lobe, is a structure called the hippocampus. As it turned out, my Bilateral Bell's Palsy was pretty much related to that part of the brain. So, with the hippocampus, this part of the brain changes all the time with memories, such as your first kiss or the birth of a child, and these memories are stored by electrical activity which is how the brain communicates.

Poor mental health is one of the biggest issues in the workplace today, causing over 70 million working days to be lost each year. [14] This includes everything from the most commonly-experienced symptoms of stress and anxiety, right through to more complex mental health conditions, such as depression, bipolar disorder and obsessive compulsive disorder. As well as having a huge impact on individual employees, poor mental health has severe repercussions for employers – including increased staff turnover, absence due to debilitating depression, burnout and exhaustion, decreased motivation and lost productivity. But while companies of all shapes and sizes increasingly understand the importance of good mental health, many simply don't feel confident handling and communicating these issues in the workplace.

As a leader, your mental well-being is vital for your team. Leaders are understandably under increased pressure to cut costs and optimise return on investment, and may not immediately understand the business impact of poor mental health. Good mental health is vital to business performance, because when staff feel happy and well cared for, they are more engaged, more motivated and more loyal. As a leader, you need on-going training and support to help handle mental health issues day to day. An effective mental health strategy considers prevention, intervention and protection. Employee benefits are a good way to provide tangible support for staff struggling with their mental health.

---

[14] https://www.mentalhealth.org.uk/sites/default/files/CR00233_Ebook_dualbranded_interactive.pdf

During my interview with Jacqui Mann, founder of J Mann associates, and author of 'Recruit, Inspire & Retain', she told me that she allocates a special time each day where she meditates away from the busy office and away from her mobile phone. She learnt this in her early stages as a hairdresser that 'Me' is more important.

Fourteen years ago we all had two domains to manage and they were our personal domain and professional domain. But around 2004, something else came into our lives, of course you know it, it is Facebook. Today, there are over 2.19 billion active users on Facebook. It might come as a surprise to you, but Linkedin has been around since 2002 and as a professional platform has 467 million active users. Compare those figures to the amount of the 7.6 billion population in the world, and 3 billion people at work according to the world employment trend, 2011. So clearly, LinkedIn still has a fair amount of offline non-users, while just under one-third of the population are using Facebook. Where am I going with those figures, you may ask. Well, since those two main platforms and some others came into our lives, we spend an average of 25 times a day looking at Facebook and about twice a day for about 20 minutes on LinkedIn. Now we are having to manage four domains instead of two: virtual personal life, non-virtual personal life, virtual professional life, and non-virtual professional life. These disruptors are part of our daily living – we go out with friends, we post on Facebook, our friends comment and we respond. We finish our work and post a trend on LinkedIn or congratulate a work colleague. We like a post while at work, or friends like ours and we use

LinkedIn while at work. Sure, we used to leave work behind at work and focus on personal time during off-work times. Are we equipped to manage this change?

If you don't use those social media, then I'm afraid you could be left behind as this new paradigm takes over the world. I have come across many leaders who do not use Facebook or are not on LinkedIn, especially amongst the baby boomers. I completely agree with them: they grew up in the age where a handshake was a contract and nothing could beat a face- to-face meeting. But if you are an echo boomer (a child of the baby boomers) and you are not using these social media, most likely to the world, you may not exist. Sadly, if that is you, I strongly suggest opening a social media account of some sort. If you have one already, take a look at how you can manage this more effectively.

Alice G Watson, who is a contributor to forbes.com,[15] pointed out six ways that social media can detrimentally affect your mental health and they are:

1. It's addictive: "Mindlessly scrolling through our social media feeds when we have a few spare minutes (or for some, hours). As we probably know intuitively, and as the research is confirming, it's not the best habit when it comes to our collective psychology."

2. It triggers sadness and less well-being: "Rather than

---

[15] https://www.forbes.com/sites/alicegwalton/2017/06/30/a-run-down-of-social-medias-effects-on-our-mental-health/#601c76c2e5af

enhancing well-being, as frequent interactions with supportive 'offline' social networks powerfully do, the current findings demonstrate that interacting on Facebook may predict the opposite result for young adults—it may undermine it."

3. More friends on social media does not necessarily mean more social friends. "A couple of years ago, a study by Royal Society Publishing [16] (http://rsos.royalsociety publishing.org/content/3/1/15029) found that more friends on social media doesn't necessarily mean you have a better social life—there seems to be a cap on the number of friends a person's brain can handle, and it takes actual social interaction (not virtual) to keep up these friendships.

4. It can lead to jealousy—and a vicious cycle. Social media creates an envious mindset which leads to jealousy because users see people on social networks who try to portray their lives as perfect; which affects their mental health negatively when they feel as though they do not meet the standards of those people's lives.

5. Cyberbullying is also a serious issue that follows social media. Social media can be a dangerous pit for any users because they are vulnerable to online harassment and bullying on any platform. Walton connects cyberbullying to "sadness" and "less well-being", implying that

[16] http://rsos.royalsocietypublishing.org/content/3/1/150292

cyberbullying can harm somebody's mental and emotional health.

6. We get caught in the delusion of thinking it will help. Part of the unhealthy cycle is that we keep coming back to social media, even though it doesn't make us feel very good. This is probably because of what's known as a forecasting error. Like a drug, we think getting a fix will help, but it actually makes us feel worse, which comes down to an error in our ability to predict our own response.

Here are my 7 action steps to manage your mental well-being:

1. Listen to your body, take regular breaks and keep active.
2. Ask for help.
3. Have regular meetings on staff well-being at work.
4. HR Zone provides a very helpful toolkit to use:
    https://www.hrzone.com/unum/wellbeing-toolkit
5. Meet people you can trust, and have a supportive network to talk about your feelings.
6. Do something you are good at.
7. Accept who you are.

Leavers to Leaders: Leading Oneself

Physical Well-Being

I remember a famous catchphrase, 'an apple a day keeps the doctor away' when I was in the military, which stayed with me forever. But what if it was true?

Now, I am not so certain about that statement, but I know for sure that if you do regular exercise, it is good for your overall well-being and brain stimulation. Dr Wendy Suzuki, a Professor of Neural Science and Psychology at the New York University Center, said it stimulates the hippocampus part of the brain, especially in contributing to better mood, energy and attention span, and this has immediate impact on your brain. The brain produces new neurons each time you exercise and protects both the pre-frontal lobe and hippocampus against future diseases. She is also the author of 'Healthy Brain, Happy Life: A Personal Program to Activate Your Brain and Do Everything Better'.

In the military, we are used to exercise first thing in the morning during training and at the time I couldn't understand why. The research was not available then, but now I can understand the positive impact that a two-mile run will have on a new trainee for better learning. I now also understand where performance comes from. So, if all that research points out that physical exercise leads to better performance, as a leader we need to pay close attention to our physical well-being.

So let's look at how we as leaders can easily manage our physical well-being and what movements would work out best for you. For me, as a sport enthusiast, as a general rule of thumb, the more muscle fibres you work, the more calories you burn. I learned these rules from the age of 14. I remember waking up and doing 25 press ups and 10 pull ups. My mum thought I was crazy, but they felt good. To this day, I wake up daily and bang 50 press ups, then move to my door frame and do 10 pulls ups. My wife thinks I am crazy and I have no idea what my daughters are thinking.

However what I have learned is that no one can be overwhelmed by a walk.

"Nobody is overwhelmed by a walk."

Sometimes, the idea of going for a run, attending a gym class or playing a team sport may seem like too much to do once you've gotten home from a hard day at work. A walk, on the other hand, is an inoffensive prospect and is easily achievable. Making time for even a half-hour jaunt won't disrupt your day; in fact, it makes me feel more vibrant for everything else in the daily grind. Anything that will increase your heart rate for at least 20 minutes a day is good for you. Perhaps 20 minutes power walk, 5 minutes core exercises or 10 minutes speed cycling. Walking is free, no membership is required. There's no off-season for walking – so long as you're appropriately dressed for the season, you can walk any day of the year (unless it rains, of course). It can be scheduled in no matter what else is in your calendar, which thus makes it easier to become a staple of your routine. I also suggest to walk without your phone, — shock, horror — and simply take in the sensual delights of your surroundings, or, you can do it with someone else. Walking provides a great opportunity to catch up with family and friends. Give it a try for a few days. What you'll get out of it far outweighs the effort required to implement it as a staple of your routine.

Set a routine, your brain needs to know this is the time to exercise. You can leave it to chance — that's what most leaders do, they plan three days a week and leave exercise to chance. If you do this, you will never have time, so it needs to be scheduled in... block it out in your diary.

During my interview with Chris Marco Flores, who served in both US and UK military and reinvented himself as a coach to cure obesity with his company Whealth: Health is the Real Wealth — this is what he had to say:

"As a leader it's vital to maintain your physical health if you want to optimise performance daily."

Just imagine if you have a car and you look after it by topping up the fluid levels, checking the tyre pressures and keeping the car clean regularly. You will be able to drive this car with very few problems for 20+ years. If you do not look after the car, then you will forever be fixing problems.

Your physical well-being is the same, it just needs different ingredients: filling your body with good nutrition daily, combined with regular exercise. This will enable you to perform at your optimal potential every day without having to rely on things like coffee or energy drinks.

Fill your body with crap and do not exercise, and you will forever be trying to find resources to keep you moving throughout the day. This is where you will see people reaching for a cup of coffee or energy drinks to keep going.

If you are in a position where your physical well-being is not so great, it is going to be incredibly tough as you begin your journey to physical health. But the great news is that once you get past the hard stage and get yourself to a good level of fitness, you will crave fitness and enjoy the benefits that you receive and it will become a part of your life.

It's very simple to achieve.

Exercise + Nutrition + Time = Great results.

There is a way to strengthen this formula, and by doing so it helps you remain focused, motivated and decreases your chances of giving up throughout the year. It takes five simple steps:

1. Mindset
2. Planning
3. Preparation
4. Exercise and nutrition

5. Challenges

Although challenges is the last step, it's the first one you should focus on. Create challenges like 5k, 10k triathlon, Three Peak Challenge, etc. By always having a challenge in place, it will help you to remain focused and it is a great way to indicate where your fitness level is. After the challenges, you will be able to know if you need to increase your fitness regime or maintain it.

There are two sides to remaining fit and healthy – exercise and nutrition – and there are 5 simple steps to take.

Exercise.

1. **Ease yourself into it** – If you haven't done fitness for a while, and go too hard too quickly, you will simply put yourself off exercising and may never continue. The best way is to ease yourself in for at least two weeks just to shake off the cobwebs and this can be as simple as going for a walk for an hour five days a week.

2. **Increase the intensity** – Now that you have shaken off the cobwebs, you will want to start increasing the intensity, so by the end it becomes slightly uncomfortable. Try to increase it a little more in every session (but do not kill yourself through these fitness sessions!) Between 4-8 weeks depending on your fitness levels.

3. **Fear the session** – At least three sessions a week, you should have a slight sense of fear before going into a

session. By having a slight sense of fear, you know it's going to be a good session and by taking on a session that you know is going to be uncomfortable, you will increase your fitness levels.

4. **Challenge yourself** – Put yourself through challenges that are literally going to challenge you. Always have a challenge: a minimum of four each year.

5. **Find something you love** – Fitness is not all about going to the gym or running for miles on end. Once you have got yourself to a fitness level that you are happy with, you must find a type of fitness that you look forward to going to, rather than it being a chore and by doing so, this will help you naturally maintain your fitness levels.

Nutrition

1. **Get motivated** – If you are trying to go from poor nutrition to good nutrition, I put people through a seven-day detox, and by doing so, you will get quick results which will motivate you mentally and it also help to flush a lot of toxins out of your body, which helps decrease the amount of sugar and caffeine you crave.

2. **Fill up your nutrition levels** – It's very important to have a good level of nutrition because when you deplete your body of nutrition for a long period of time, the system in your body will stop running as fluidly. So by filling your body with the right nutrition, it starts helping

your body to function in the correct way.

3. **Manipulate your diet** – Once your nutrition levels are filled and your system is starting to run better, then you can manipulate your diet until you get your body the way you need and want it to be, which could be to lose fat or gain muscle.

4. **Turn it into a lifestyle** – There are literally so many types of healthy nutrition methods. Go through different methods until you can find one that fits your lifestyle and discover what works best for your body. (Just like Step 5 for Exercise).

Leavers to Leaders: Leading Oneself

Financial Well-Being

I have included this chapter in this book purely because most people usually decide to make a change, or do something different, when they experience more 'pain' than they can handle – the desire to get away from their current situation is so strong that they are almost forced to make the change and find a new job. When I decided to remove myself from full-time service In the British Armed Forces to become a reservist, I had a plan. I bought my house a few months before I was due to leave the military. At that time, I had a daughter (who was nearly one year old) and my wife to support. This was the start of a huge period of life-changing learning, beginning with the realisation of 'more money' being my main driver – which is what I thought I was aiming for. However, money is simply a by-product of success. The main things all this is really about are freedom and choice.

It is very unlikely you will move straight into another job or career, but if things take their time and you are in a gap or still in the process to revolutionise yourself and go where your heart takes you, you will need to have a grip on your finances.

As you position yourself as an entrepreneurial leader, you will also more likely have to work within a budget, or be advising your boss about business finance. What better way to deal with finance than by dealing with your own personal finances – be your own financial adviser. We are all responsible for our own financial wellbeing, not the government. Where I grew up and other developing countries, you have to put food on the table, go to work and sustain your family. State benefits are there only if the main partner dies and the family needs support. If you become unemployed, you usually have to carry on meeting your mortgage/rent costs and utility bills.

Firstly, you will have to develop a good understanding of your needs and how you might go about meeting them. According to the United Kingdom Financial Services Authority [17] survey of June 2018, 49% of people in England, 54% in Wales and 55% of the population in Scotland are not good at managing money or are in difficulty and vulnerable to debt.

It is important at this stage to be able to manage your own personal finances. There is no need to run to a financial adviser to run your day-to-day life. They may come in handy at a later stage, but for now you can always get a DIY book or online programme to tabulate your income vs expenses.

I am not a personal adviser, and I don't intend to become one either, but the one thing I have come across which can be beneficial to anyone – especially since the statistics are very strong about it – is managing your personal finances. For some of you, this might be less necessary, depending on how you exit your current job. The circumstances are always different for everyone.

---

[17] https://www.fca.org.uk/publication/research/financial-lives-consumers-across-uk.pdf

There are no bad ways of managing money, but there are always bad ways to mismanage money. For me personally, it has always worked to live on 70% of my income. Based on an average earning of £25,000 after tax and national insurance, if you can pinch 10% (£48 a week), you will have an extra £2,500 a year. If you invest that for two years at 6%, you will have £5,291. This is your first jar: this money is for investment only or for anything that is an asset and goes up in value. In this first example, I used two years specifically because this is about the right amount of time for you to revolutionise yourself if your current job is not heading anywhere. My point is also to show you how small change makes a big difference.

So we mentioned earlier about living on 70 percent of your household income. So what do we do with the remaining 20 percent?

The next 10% is for your charity/gift or donation which you use to support your chosen organisation. I have to admit that I always struggled with this one in my early years until I personally experienced and understood that there is more joy in giving than receiving. Do you remember the last time you helped someone – how did you feel?

Lastly, we have another 10 percent that goes into your fun account. It is called fun because this is literally the idea of this account; you have to spend it . You can choose to spend it weekly, monthly or even yearly on a vacation, but the money is there to spend.

This means you also need to have a good grip on other expenses or debts. This chapter is not to deal with debt, but if this is your case, visit Dave Ramsey's website www.daveramsey.com or get his book 'The Money Makeover' on Amazon. Like many things in life, a little careful planning and preparation (and a dash of cunning) are required to navigate your work transition. As you plan such change to make a palpable difference to your pockets and future leadership career, you have to incorporate this into your own lifestyle as soon as you can – and this is the purpose of this whole book.

Incorporating just a handful of thrifty tricks and a little financial savvy, by living on 70% of your earnings month by month, will allow you to pick up money-saving skills that will last a lifetime. By the end of the year, you will have saved several thousands of pounds on food, clothing, household expenses and travel costs. These changes will help you to focus on your next big job or career and enjoy some relaxation time before you start your new one.

I am hoping this simple strategy can help you live a life where you can have more control over your money. If you are in doubt, I strongly recommend seeking the help of a personal adviser, or a friend who is a bit better with finances than you. The idea of this exercise is for you to get used to cutting your costs and living on less income. You can always rename those jars as you wish, but you will still have 30 percent of savings to use. The final aim is for you to have at least three months of your monthly wages in savings for when you transition.

Here is what Yannick Koo Seen Lin, CPA, CGMA, MBA, Owner and CEO of KSL – who has also had to reinvent himself several times and now runs a global company in Mauritius and Australia – has to say about managing personal finance:

"The same principle of managing a corporate entity applies to managing personal finance. In essence, cash is the life-blood which keep an organisation alive. An organisation can be viewed as highly successful in terms of high turnover, high profits and high potential for growth. Nevertheless, without the flowing of cash to meet its obligations, the organisation is artificially successful and is doomed to crash. The same analogy can be applied to personal finance. Cash is a fundamental element in managing a successful household. Success is not defined by what can be seen by the eyes, like owning luxurious cars, possessing luxurious properties and having a high-profile position. It would be meaningless if those have been acquired on unhealthy debts and the inability to pay off those debts. At the end of day, it is the cash position which defines the successful running of a household."

The 7 action steps to manage your financial well-being:

1. Budget: Identify what your income is and spend less than you earn.
2. Know: Distinguish between needs and wants.
3. Consultation: take into account your partner's opinion.
4. Save: Put aside 10-15% of your salary as rain money.
5. Plan: Consider your future needs.
6. Invest: Look at wise investment.
7. Review: Constantly reassess your personal finance strategy.

Leavers to Leaders: Leading Oneself

The Two V's: Vision and Being Vital

When Disney World first opened, Mrs Walt Disney was asked to speak at the grand opening, because Walt had died. She was introduced by a man who said, "Mrs Disney, I just wish Walt could have seen this." She stood up and said, "He did," and sat down. Walt knew it! What we see is what we get.

During my time in the military, I have grasped the concept of vision very well. You see, this is the one thing we plan well and there is always a contingency plan. I remember during training, we would plan an attack by using models. The ground and environment have been shaped and the plan of attack has been discussed. You could see the target, you could see the aim.

In leading oneself, you need to be able to vision your life. I have come across a lot of people who simply drift though life, they don't plan anything and spend a lot of time wishing. I have never been a big fan of buying Lottery tickets, but it is always a good story when you read about someone winning millions. Still I will not buy a single ticket. I remember in the 80s as I grew up, one of the regular questions I would get asked by my uncles was, "How are your studies? You need to work hard to achieve your dreams." What they didn't know is that I only had one dream: my dream was to be like them. They were both close protection police officers at the time to the Mauritius Prime Minister. But that vision of riding fast speed bikes, beside a man in a black suit in a black Mercedes had always been with me. Today I have a fleet of black limos as part of our chauffeur service run by ex-military personnel.

A vision will take you a long way. There is a well-known quote in the Bible: "Where there is no vision, the people perish"[18].

Planning however is only a result of vision; vision is a simple activity of the mind. Visualisation of something is the key.

16 PLANNING IS A RESULT OF VISION

As you lead yourself, having a personal vision for your life is vital. When I look around now that I am in my 40s, I see a lot of people who build a career then coast from 40 to 65. Now that's a long time to coast. I also see service leavers starting a new career, and most of the time they are at full speed. The problem

---

[18] Proverbs 29:18

is when you are coasting, you are comfortable and off guard, you relax, and anything can knock you over. I see this scenario over and over.

To this day, I still have my 2001 diary. I had a vision and it was not just about moving to London and seeing that some of the roads are painted red, and living the dream. It actually was not that straightforward moving to England, especially living in London, where you cannot step outside without spending a penny. I can remember each time when a thought or belief occurred to me out of the blue, I would write it down. Because life is not always a dream.

By 2004, we bought our very first house. I remember how we still had friends living in the married quarters. At the time, it was hard for me having to lose those friendships and move into our new house. It was my dad's work ethic that made me buy a home in UK; he had a vision. His first job was as a bread distributor in his village in Quatre Soeurs. Mauritius inherited this French habit of eating fresh baguettes every day. So every day before school, he would deliver bread and cycle about 5km each way to distribute bread. He also became the first person in his village to join the police force and later was joined by his two younger brothers. He worked hard and built his own house so we could have our own place.

Vision breeds opportunity. If you don't have a vision, every opportunity will pass you by. Remember the words: Opportunity is nowhere or Opportunity Is now here.

Now that we all understand the importance of having a vision, let's take a look at the other 'V' – being Vital. Cambridge Dictionary describes vital as: "necessary for the success or continued existence of something; extremely important."

However, the best description I have is from Daniel Priestley's book, 'Key Person of Influence' and to understand the concept, we also need to understand another term he used, which is, 'functional'. Functional people might be great at what they do, they might talk the talk and walk the walk, but the harsh reality is they are performing a role that is replaceable. If someone can find a cheaper option they will take it, because a functional person is just one possible solution to a problem. On the other side, a vital leader is someone who contributes to the success of the organisation. This person is missed and people cry for them when they are not at work. The world is changing and if you want to be this type of person, then you need to become a vital person that cannot be replaced.

Remember the Deloitte report on the future of work: if you are earning £30k and work in London, in the next 10 years your job is most likely to be replaced. What that means for you as a leaver in transition, is that you need to become more vital. Most organisations now look for entrepreneurial people; these skills cannot be automated, Being vital is being entrepreneurial. During our case study, most of the interviewees acknowledged this skill at an early stage of their career journey. Jacqui was more than an admin person in her recruitment job, she became vital, and this quality enabled her to learn more about HR and she later found a job with an American firm. I had the same experience in the military, I saw a need to support the regiment and became a linguist. I have no doubt that my peers were jealous of me as being the CO military liaison is a dream work for a Lance Corporal.

As we close this chapter of Leading Oneself, see yourself as a vital person, visualise your position and start acting and performing as a vital person.

You will know your role in the organisation, next time you get back from a holiday, by how much the work place has been missing you. Others when they go on a holiday, no one seems to notice. That is the sign of a functional person. Have a vision. Be vital. Become entrepreneurial.

Here are the 7 action steps to become more visionary and vital:

1. Prioritise You.
2. Delegate more.
3. Empower others and impact their lives.
4. Develop a positive mindset and talk in the present tense.
5. Have a higher vision for your life and career.
6. Adopt an attitude of serving others.
7. Be overly grateful about yourself and others.

CHAPTER 6

Leavers to Leaders Lead Others

Leading Generations

In this chapter we will use our P.R.I.D.E model to explain the process of leading others. Being at a very interesting phase of mankind, with five different generations in the workplace, we will firstly look at each of these generations and how to lead them and their needs, what motivates them, how they communicate and how they see the world. Most importantly, we'll look at how to lead a multi-generational workplace.

Predominantly, we have the traditionalists who will be those born before 1945, followed by the largest generation the baby boomers, and their children, the Gen X or Generation X (those born between 1965 to 1980). This is followed by the second largest population, the Generation Y, also known as millennials, born between 1980-1990 and Generation Z, born post-1990. If you look around the workplace you will most likely identify at least the three main generations which are baby boomers, Gen

X, and millennials. In the next five to ten years we will also see a shift in the workplace with more Gen Y reaching out to high or senior roles, while more Gen Z will be entering the workplace. Your role in leading others is to serve them, and unless you take the time and create an environment for each of the above generations to co-work, your job can be very difficult to retain any of them, especially the millennials and Gen Z.

So why are generations different?

Well, each of the above generation are at different ages and were born in different conditions of time, which means they each have had varied experiences, which you can attribute to how they see themselves. However, age is not the sole reason for generational behaviours, otherwise teenagers today would not be distinguishable from teenagers from previous generations.

It's also about the current economic, political and social conditions which we all live under that further divide the generations. The same conditions act upon people of different ages in different ways – a good example is Marc Prensky, best known as the inventor and populariser of the terms "digital native" and "digital immigrant". Whilst everyone can send a text or download a podcast, Gen Y have been exposed to these in their formative years and so the digital language and technology is almost their first language.

During my LOS talk with Captain Brian Hamel, Commander of USS Gunston Hall LSD 44, on managing millennials, he pointed out that 90% of his team were millennials and how he has to make sure to reward them accordingly across the board. He successfully leads his ship based on three principles: honesty, humbleness and humour.

Experiences that occur during formative childhood and teenage years also create and define differences between the generations. These social markers produce the paradigms through which the world is viewed. These three elements contribute to create generational attributes and let's take a look at each one of them:

Baby boomers:

We have all heard of the baby boomers – they were the most spoken about generation after World War Two. They are so big as a generation that everything they touch becomes global news – from investment, to property, pensions, vacations and finally, medical care. They had such impact on each of these industries that they almost disrupted them. It is widely reported that about 10,000 of them are retiring daily, so hence the surge of vacations and medical costs. This also brings about some drawbacks with them selling their properties and investments, and as we have found out, the next generation are not too bothered about buying or actually owning. We have seen how shared ownership is becoming the norm already in the hospitality and transport industry. In the past, if most of them are aware of the future of work, they are now likely to become advisors or NED (non-executive director) on many SME and small companies, as long as they learn to blend into the next generations of Xers and millennials. Boomers tend to be tolerant if they are well-managed, the same as the Xers who have inherited this forced habit but end up being unhappy and unmotivated. Over the years, they have preferred an academic learning or science base, and their generation created a culture of long working hours. Boomers have also been the loyal generation to employment. I can personally relate to that when I look at my dad who worked for twenty years as a police officer as well as his own dad.

50^s ~ 70^s ~ 90^s ~ 2000^s

17......"4 GENERATIONS,... THROUGH THE AGES!!"

Generation X

Generation Xers are perhaps the middle or the bridge generation as I call them. They have seen and lived through at least two recessions in the UK — 1999 and the 2008 global meltdown. They have seen and experienced the hardship of their parents, the baby boomers, and also seen the rise of automation and are the most ready to adapt to change. They are not naturally tech savvy, but they understand technology and, most importantly, can adapt to it. They were reluctantly working the long hours set by the boomers and certainly don't want to be in stressful jobs like their parents, working long hours. This is the generation we see in the workplace today in their 40s. As a generation, they are very quiet, unlike the millennials. They tend to be shy with social media, however they are the generation which is ready to lead, and they have certainly learnt a lot from their previous generation, the boomers, and also understand the next generation better than their peers. They appreciate good leadership, structured training and personal development led by experts and they strive for a good work-life balance. They understand what makes their generation tick and are ready to act upon their understanding should they realise their value and position in the workplace. Just like the boomers, they consider a drink with their friends a social space. Gen X understand the helicopter approach to leadership, an analogy we will explore better in the next chapter. As such, they are the ideal generation to be head of HR, team leader and managing the organisation, and most importantly bridging the gap between those three main generations. Bringing new change and development, they promote a culture of work-life balance. In the past, they have already seen poor management, lack of support, poor motivation and less recognition. They want a change and are ready to adapt.

Millennials and Gen Z

Millennials form the youngest generation in the workforce to usher in a new employment trend. These young workers value personal downtime and have no desire to be the "company people" their parents (Gen X) were. They will simply not put up with it and will resign.

Human resource managers whose companies lack work-life balance programmes, or "cool" brands, must be ready to lobby for greater scheduling flexibility and social responsibility in the workplace to attract and hire millennials. They want to use their strengths and be trusted to do their best. After millennials are hired, HR must find out how to earn their loyalty to prevent chronic turnover that leads to costly rehiring. This generation highly values personal time, and can quickly text and tweet between work assignments and leisure activities. They prefer to learn from their peers, coaching and mentoring using fun and multi-sensory experiences. Another HR task is to reduce tensions among baby boomers, Generation Xers and millennials in the workplace and train them to work as team members. One of the mistakes of recruiters and HR is to assume that this generation like online learning like the previous two generations and stereotype them because they are more tech savvy. Social space for them is when they are on their social media and not at the pub. Working does not have to be 9-5 for millennials. They would be happy to stay at home and do the same work in the same time as long as it is on their own terms. Many students I come across during my mentorship programme want a leader who can motivate them to pursue their passion, align with a good culture and can push them forward in their career.

As the demographic composition of the workforce changes, their motivations and expectations evolve too. It is imperative that HR understands what is most valued by these workers. Is it compensation, or prestige, or perhaps autonomy at work? In many cases, HR will have to adapt their incentives, benefits policies, and retention strategies for workers that are not just driven by financial compensation. It is not enough simply to recruit able staff. Companies have to make sure that their people are committed, productive, and do not leave after a short period, incurring substantial turnover costs and wasting all previous training invested in them.

Here are the 7 steps in leading generations:

1. Treat everyone differently according to their generation. Never assume that people are the same.
2. Praise when praise is due, especially on the smallest things – just like a Facebook like means a lot to some people.
3. Understand each value for each generation. What motivates one generation may not necessarily work for the other.
4. Create your team in a way to mix generations together on problem solving.
5. Everyone is looking for a work-life balance, and the sooner you can create this environment, the happier the team will be.
6. Understand the workplace has changed and as a leader you role is to help the generations to perform together. This can also be achieved with the help of outside consultant.
7. Gen Xers are the middle generation and can sometimes be seen as bridging the gap between baby boomers and millennials – get them involved where possible.

Leavers to Leaders Leading Others

Promote

In this chapter we will use our P.R.I.D.E model to explain the process of leading others. The first letter P in Pride stands for 'promote' and as we aim to help our team to better performance, it helps to better understand them, their values, their goals and ambitions. Our role is to predict the future not dwell on the past. One of the key elements of leading others in the work place is to promote their wellbeing and get better input from your team. A leader that does not see the value and talent of its employees, does not last long anyway. The role of a leader is to identify the value of his people and encourage them to go further.

We are currently at a very interesting time on earth because for the very first time in human life, we have five generations in the workplace at the same time, unintentionally. On one hand we have the baby boomers entering retirement, on another hand we have the Gen X and millennials entering into leadership role in the workplace. It is time we get a bit more intentional about how we work collectively. Each of these generations come with their own ways of upbringing and mode de vie. We are in a world where we really need to be more aware of the people we lead. A number of European studies have shown that age-diverse teams are more effective and successful, however only about 8% of companies have a diversity inclusion programme and have expanded this programme to include age as just as important of a demographic as gender or race. For the modern workplace to become more effective, we need to open up those intergenerational pipelines of wisdom, so that we can learn from each other. In the US, almost 40% of the workplace have a boss that is younger than them and that number is growing quickly. The power is cascading like never before because of our increasing reliance on digital intelligence.

In 2018, we honoured the 100th year since 1.3 million sailors, soldiers and airmen from the Hindu, Sikh and Muslim countries served together with bravery and distinction to defend British interest around the world in the First World War. This has led to many settling in the country and forming a new British-Asian community. To this day, the British Armed forces includes its Commonwealth citizens in recruitment and I am here because I am one of them. My grandfather also served with the logistics team in North Africa during World War Two. I remember looking at his pictures on the wall when we visited him and how he always spoke about it with great respect. We were also happy to be getting our Christmas presents from his army pension.

Hence the reason why the British Armed Forces is the number one organisation at managing diversity in the work place. During my service, although I was a rare Mauritian national to join, I also made some great and lifelong friends from Scotland, Ireland, and many other Commonwealth countries. Today, managing diversity in the workplace is not just about culture, as much as it is also about respecting the ways of life of each individual. Diversity also comes from the different age groups, values and social preferences. When it comes to power in the workplace today, 30 is the new 50. As you lead others, this becomes a fundamental part of your organisation. As a leader you could be working in a business-to-business, business-to-customer, customer-to-customer world, but the business is and has always been in the H2H (human-to-human) world.

IS AS A LEADER, iT HAS ALWAYS BEEN iN THE H2H (HUMAN TO HUMAN) WORLD!!

Being relevant in the workplace is important, the ability to use timeless wisdom and apply it to modern-day problems. The baby boomers should be seen in a non-executive capacity, almost as providing mentorship to the team, Gen X and baby boomers are important for the success of the team. I still find that lack of integration in the work place in many organisations and even in churches where you would expect a better integration and multi-generational community. To effectively manage diversity in the work place, it will be up to the leader to set the example and the military is excellent at it, as it comes from the top. So how do you promote diversity in the workplace?

Dr Nigel Paterson has given a number of presentations in the past, often focusing on the management of business communication across human differences. His ongoing training work in business and cross-cultural communication, given both in the UK and overseas, brings him into contact with a range of business people, charity professionals, politicians and government officers.

'Many of us would like to have more influence on the people around us. Influence is distinguished here from the privileges and possibilities of managing those responsible to us,' says Nigel.

Diversity is taken here to refer to the great variation that is to be found among people who are different from each other because of age, nationality, ethnicity, social background, beliefs and gender. It is all too easy to stick around people like ourselves.

There is a huge potential for diverse teams in the workplace. It can mean a wider pool of ideas, approaches and understanding, and more opportunity for profit in our multicultural world. There is scope for a lot of fun in the workplace too, maybe getting to know different kinds of people who we could hardly picture when at school.

Diversity is not a fad, likely to be replaced by something else in a few years time. It's all about people and relating to them better.

The flip side of this is that unmanaged diversity can be a big problem, even inside companies with well-meaning managers. People who are widely different from one another are not suddenly going to get on with each other just because they are thrown together. Diverse teams do not automatically do well. Managing diversity needs humility and an on-going readiness to keep learning from others.

To better understand the impact of diversity, let's take for example one of the largest and well-known companies on earth, Google. Google released its 2018 annual diversity report and the percentage of female employees rose by .1 percent to 30.9 percent. The percentage of Asian employees grew by 1.3 percent to 36.3 percent and the percentage of black and Latina employees by .1 percent to 2.5 percent and 3.6 percent respectively. Danielle Brown, chief diversity and inclusion officer at Google says, if we want a better outcome, we need to evolve our approach. So managing diversity is an ongoing issue according to Google – even though they are doing quite a good job at it, it remains a priority.

Having travelled around the world, this unfortunately is a common mismanagement I observe and this is a main chapter at TriExForces. We have a Chinese operations director, a black director and a female managing director, and I am looking forward to the day we have a female CEO to take over and lead the group globally. As Britain exits Europe, I am hoping for more business opportunities between the colonies and already we can see deals from Australia coming to the UK and hence engaging businesses and organisations once again in a global market. As leaders, and as we enter 2020, we will be called to better manage diversity and to value different cultures and it does require some thought and skill in doing so.

If in doubt, I strongly recommend taking a look at how the Ministry of Defence manages diversity in the workplace, which according to its 2017 report, looks like this:

Ages 50-59:	39.7 percent
Ages 40-49:	24.6 percent
Ages 30-39	7.3 percent
Ages 16-29:	7.3 percent
Female representation:	42 percent
BAME Black, Asian, ethnic minority:	4.6 percent
LGB Lesbian, Gay & Bisexual:	2.1 percent
Christian:	67 percent
Non Christian:	5.3 percent
Secular:	27 percent

Here are 7 action steps to manage a multi-diversity generation in the work place:

1. Recognise the need to train and create a model that will embrace the intergeneration team and mix and match them into a sub-group.
2. Report shows that some generations will stay in a job for a least two years and millennials are expected to have ten jobs by the age of 38. Promote from within.
3. Understand the gap and bridge the gap with leaders who can understand multi-generations.
4. Become a role model for others and have good mentors and good managers to support you.
5. Review the workplace culture and values as often as possible to appeal to all generations.
6. Continue to monitor in finding out what makes your team tick.
7. Raise awareness for your key managers, the board and the trustees which will help them understand this issue of a multi-generational workforce.

Leavers to Leaders Leading Others

Reward

Leading others is still the hardest part of the job. People make or break an organisation. What type of people you want to have is one of the greatest challenges. As leaders, hiring good people can also be the most difficult aspect of our jobs. However, good hiring decisions can also yield the most rewards. When looking to hire folks for your team, it is important to not only consider a candidate's skillset and past experience, but also what they can bring to the team in IQ and emotional intelligence.

The military hierarchy system is perhaps the best at this. I remember as a young junior non-commissioner officer (JCNO), looking up to the second lieutenant who actually just took his role as troop commander. But even the young second lieutenant is never alone in his leadership role, he/she is surrounded by more experienced folks – normally a Warrant officer who has been in the military for years and knows how to manage the day-to-day of the military but also managing others. The success of my team is always a result of having team members who are better than me and who can challenge the assumptions or dismantle the notion, "but that is how we do it here".

The best performing teams are those who possess the confidence to challenge the status quo, think strategically and speak up in order to put the success of the organisation at the forefront of every decision. It is sometimes difficult to separate what we hear from our feelings about the person who says it. Non-existent motives may be ascribed to the communicator. If we like someone, we are more likely to accept what he says – whether it is right or wrong – than if we dislike him. The same applies to the team. They are more likely to listen to their colleagues who share their experiences, than to outsiders and anyone who will challenge the norms. Some messages have to be in writing to get the message across promptly and without any variations in the way they are delivered. But, wherever possible, supplementing written messages with spoken words can be much more effective. Your job is to facilitate this environment of communication.

Right from the outset, when hiring a team, I am drawn to innovators. Simply put, they are willing to try new things: the 'why not' people. I once hired a consultant to help with the planning of the business but failed to outline the importance of 'why not', and we soon discovered the culture clash between our businesses. At 'Tri', it can have a lot of meaning. In the military, it means the joint operations of the British Army, Royal Navy, Royal Air Force and Royal Marines. But for us, it is about making an effort to serve at our very best and that is what Tri means to us.

So hiring smart, innovative people is only half of the equation. Keeping them engaged and their skills sharp requires work. From my experience, the best way to foster this type of focus and dedication is to really get to know them. This is done by developing lasting and meaningful relationships with them.

Listen to them, find out their passions and concerns and understand how they envision their professional growth and development. Leading others is to deepen your bond and breed loyalty. The military focuses a lot on that. First of all, most service personnel tend to live within 100 metres of each other; each rank has a mess where they meet up regularly, and the families and children know each other. At work, career development is a continuous key contribution for the personnel lives. Military people have to shift from one place to another quite regularly and having those welfare structures in place really helps in staying focused. The key to leading a successful organisation is developing a team that contributes to the best of their ability. In 2004, my regiment wanted to develop a stronger relationship with its equivalent of the French maritime military, and as a JNCO I knew I could bring more value to the table. I did so by offering my services, although I was not trained, as a professional military linguist. This however led me to qualify and enter into full-time training as a linguist to further my knowledge. In this case, it was the CO (commanding officer) who recognised the value and my ability. I soon saw myself as a military liaison with the French army, a skill that does not normally apply to JNCO. At one time, we recreated the D-Day Landing in Normandy, which took a lot of effort and work, but it was possible due to my ability to sharpen my skills.

During my case study on this chapter, I interviewed Jacqui Mann, who is the founder of J. Mann Associates, an HR outsourcing company providing HR and business support to entrepreneurs. Jacqui is better known as the 'people doctor' and is also the author of 'Recruit, Inspire & Retrain' where she talks about her six steps to recruit, retrain and create the right culture. Jacqui reinvented herself from a hairdresser to now being a published author, speaker and advisor. What really drew me to her leadership skill, is that she is also a military spouse. This is what Jacqui has to say about managing others:

"Developing and rewarding others is key for your success as a leader. You need to understand some people are better at technology and others aren't, some want more financial rewards while others want more learning development. Same goes with the clients, some have lots of coaching in the business and we are learning to adapt our training to them."

Leading others by surrounding yourself with smart and driven people who are just that – smart and driven – will enable you to develop a culture that yields a great deal of success. Is it important to identify strategies for growing and nurturing relationships and the three elements in allowing them to grow are: time, effort and imagination. So rather than focusing on academic skills, foster a system to improve the soft skills[19] of the team and activities to develop trust among employees. Empower them to lead and make decisions and eliminate unnecessary work. So much admin work can be automated these days.

We have a team that does all our calls in our Mauritius office

---

[19] **Soft skills** are a combination of people skills, social skills, communications skills, character traits, attitude, career attributes, social intelligence and emotional intelligence.

while we focus on day-to-day management of the team in UK. I have set up a daily 'group hug' at 10.30 BST where we all have a 30-minute call on Skype or Zoom, to set up the daily task. We have created a system where the satellite team feels part of the bigger vision. They do all our contents and brochures, and we print them in the UK.

As a young man growing up in Mauritius, I have always found those older than me more interesting to hang out with in the playground. I remember as a child growing up in the married quarters. It was ten times as much fun to play with the elder boys and they could come up with some great ideas. We once built a shop by the road to sell sweets. Of course, no one bought anything as we ate it all. To this day, I find myself surrounded by those who are perhaps ten times more educated than me, wiser and much older than me, and perhaps also more fun than me. I have come to realise the knowledge they possess will take me a lifetime to learn and I may not have a lifetime of learning. The baby boomers have a lot to teach us, as long as we value their time, and they can bring a lot of value and experience as you lead others, especially in the area of staff development.

Our next chapter is about involving others to lead after you set the path for them to take and bring your organisation to the next level.

Here are the 7 action steps to prepare yourself to reward others:

1. Take a holistic approach when recruiting new staff.
2. Allow your team to challenge the status quo.
3. Delegate to your subordinates and allow them to make errors.
4. Get to know your team on an individual level and get to know your team as a group.
5. Surround yourself with people who are diverse and multi-generational to better understand each of them.
6. Have a "group hug" daily or weekly calls where others can take a lead and feel rewarded.
7. Become a lifelong learner.

Leavers to Leaders: Leading Others

Involve Others to Lead

One of the common trends in the military is Continuing Professional Development (CPD). Right from the outset, you have a career ladder in front of you. For example, as a JNCO you have your eye on the next level or rank which will bring you more responsibility and financial reward. The process of moving ranks can also be very transitional; in most cases it will mean joining a new regiment to start your new role. This is because it can be hard to lead those who were previously at the same level as you. Moving to a new regiment allows you to use your new rank in a different environment and with a different team. It doesn't always work like this, as some ranks are fortunate to be stationed together for the duration of their careers. I once asked the US Navy Admiral, Gene Black, the commander of Carrier Strike Group 8, what it takes to become an Admiral, and he said that studies showed that it is not the top of the navy class who become Admiral, but the middle performers who strive harder and have the grit to get to the top.

As a leader, your job is to prepare others to lead by getting them involved in more senior roles in your organisation. I often see junior staff in attendance at some of the meetings I go to. This tells me that this organisation cares about the on-going training of their junior staff. Admiral Gene Black would often facilitate his junior officers to contribute their ideas first before hearing from his seniors, as they are the ones delivering the results and also tend to respect the opinions of their seniors.

Culture-building is one of the most important things we can do: it defines who we are as a company, helps us attract and retain the best employees and helps set us apart in the marketplace. It gives our customers a sense of who we are, how we work and ultimately what we stand for.

Quality of leadership is the most important determinant of

employee engagement. Imagine the long-term effect of sending the signal that the company insists that every employee should be working for an excellent leader. Imagine the effect of practising zero tolerance for inappropriate behaviour on the part of leaders.

It is a reflection of ourselves. Earlier, we discussed the importance of promoting diversity and managing a multi-generation culture in the workplace. In doing so, you also set the tone of the company for others to follow, but the following items are also important to help others to lead:

Vision:

To understand the company values and practices, like ethics, integrity, respect, commitment and dependability.

Mission:

A clear mission statement created jointly by the team is better understood than one created by an external consultant.

Values:

1. **Trustworthy:** We are honest and ethical. We are committed to always acting with the best of intentions for our customers, partners and colleagues.
2. **Respectful:** We pride ourselves on treating our customers, partners and colleagues with dignity and respect. We listen with an open mind. We welcome and embrace diverse experiences and perspectives in order to

deliver the very best solutions.

3. **Collaborative:** We solve problems and create solutions as a team. Whether it's working jointly with customers, partners or other teams across the organisation and satellite officers, we know teamwork always delivers the very best outcomes.

4. **Innovative:** We continually put our expertise and creativity to work to stay ahead of the curve and find new ways to solve the toughest problems our customers face.

5. **Accountable:** We stand behind our customers, partners and each other to deliver the best solutions. We work tirelessly to meet the commitments we've set forth.

6. **Relentless:** We are driven by a customer-first orientation that motivates our teams to never give up. We work tirelessly to improve our customer relationships, the solutions we deliver and our company as a whole.

Our Leadership Qualities:

1. **How We Operate** – we are accountable and results-orientated.

2. **How We Engage with Others** – we have a system to build teamwork and collaboration.

3. **How We Communicate** – we are authentic, candid and transparent in our communications.

4. **How We Act** – we take initiative, act boldly and take calculated risks to achieve success.

5. **How We Execute** – we work with speed, quality, integrity and pride.

By involving others to lead, whether it is the planning of the Christmas party, leading a project or taking on a new role, not only do you free up a lot of your time but you also allow them to see their real value in the workplace.

I was once asked to raise some money for a charity which wanted to honour its elderly members with an evening dinner. Since it was going to be low budget, the only way to add value was to delegate to people who had influence. We soon found out that the secretary's husband was a chef, another was good at decoration and another was a DJ. Soon, with lots of preparation and within a low budget (raised by washing cars), we were able to host the event.

These days, many experienced leaders are entering retirement; 10,000 baby boomers every day. In many meetings and networking events that I attend, I find myself surrounded by experienced and knowledgeable people. Sometimes buying them a cup of coffee and learning about their mistakes can be of great value. My point is, involve these people in your organisation, possibly as non-executive directors. This could be a great way for you to learn from them. Involve yourself and your team with people of value; life is too short to reinvent the wheel in business.

Also, significantly increase the number of promotions from within. Most organisations go outside for at least a third of their executive positions. Consider reducing that to a fifth. While there is value in adding an outside perspective, or filling the need for an entirely new skillset, the data clearly indicates that the failure rate of external hires is far higher than those from within. So invest in your people and promote from within.

In his book, *29 Leadership Secrets*, Jack Welch says, "Listen to the people who actually do the work." When you develop others to lead, you will be empowering them and giving yourself more time to focus on other things. We will expand on this in the next chapter, Leading Organisation.

The three types of people to be involved in your life as a leader:

People you can help, people who can help you, people you enjoy.

In this chapter, we will learn from Errol Lawson, author, mentor and entrepreneur who is passionate about leadership development: "You need to appreciate the diversity of thought from generation to generation. The collective intelligence in a team is much greater than what you can provide individually. Create a space for individuals to express themselves, their thoughts, their ideas and opinions in a safe way; an environment for open communication."

Here are the 7 action steps for you to involve others:

1. Involve the junior team on a major project, and ask their opinions.
2. Delegate and step back so others can be involved.
3. Outsource some of your less complicated work so you can focus on the team.
4. Create a system to raise the profile of the team.
5. Don't be afraid to make mistakes; managing people is still the hardest task.
6. Engage in regular team-building exercises.
7. Revisit the needs of the team as part of their future expectations.

Leavers to Leaders: Leading Others

Defend

Earlier in Chapter 5, we looked at the importance of wellbeing in leading oneself. As a leader you lead people. The military has mastered this concept for generations. Hence, at most levels you have a minimum of three people: from JNCO to NCO you have four ranks; from NCO to SNCO you have another three ranks; from SNCO to Major you have another four ranks. The military concept has always been about teamwork and cannot function except as a team. To maintain teamwork and efficiency of each member, each head is responsible for the rest. In this chapter, we first examine how we are expected to lead people as individuals, and how to create an environment for them to perform at a group level. In doing so, we also find out how the military is not made up by people... the military is the people: living, breathing, serving human beings who have needs, interests and desires. They have spirit, will, strength and abilities. They also have weaknesses and faults. We will use the term P.R.I.D.E to define the value your team contributes and show how it gets the best performance.

As we enter the world of automation, high technology and high demand, it is way too easy to treat your team as little more than a job description, as tools. When I look at big corporate, I see rows of people sitting next to each other, but barely talking to each other. As a matter of fact, studies show that a lot of those people feel lonelier at work and depression in the workplace is rising. Your role as a leader is to realise that people at all levels are people; they have a life, values, and you have to engage and lead the whole person.

So, the first letter in defend is "D". Taking care of your team is to create an environment where they can perform, learn and grow. Jacqui Mann, known as the people doctor, says she takes time to form a relationship and gets to know her staff and fits in regular sessions with them to see where they are at in the workplace. Since we are leading people, it is not a surprise to see "people skills" being at the top of the list. As a leader, you need to be able to communicate, supervise, mentor and counsel each and every member of your team.

As Jacqui says, she spends a lot of time as the doctor counselling people in the business, and often finds out it is lack of communication that is the root cause of problems. I am an advocate that the military is a great stepping stone in life; the line of communication exists and is a solid line between a JNCO to the CO. Back in 2001, I was offered a role with the infantry and after my phase one training, I realised I had achieved the top of my physical ability. Training with the paras meant you had to run 1.5 miles in under 8 minutes and I had achieved that. However, I found myself in a circle where it was hard to progress. I used my line of command to request a transfer to a more challenging role. The troop's commander and the officer in command were very well aware of my request. Unfortunately, they wanted me to stay within my role. I don't think it was common in those days to write to the CO, but that's what I did. Within two days, I was invited to his office and as it turned out, he was very impressed by my courage to reach out to him. The interview was not what I was expecting: it was the very first time I got invited to speak with a Lieutenant Colonel. I remember being very scared and I stood in attention, waiting to be called into his office, but I had my emotion in check. When I walked into his office, he looked at my file, saw that I was from Mauritius and said: "Vous parlez francais?" I thought I heard wrong. I was shocked! To which I responded "Oui Monsieur." The next 15 minutes was a casual conversation between two human beings. We ended the meeting with a handshake and I was on my way to the next regiment. During my time in the military, I have found that in the end even the most high-ranking officers are human beings; I have never felt intimidated by them and to this date I have some great professional relationships with some of most respectable military personnel both in UK and around the world.

As a leader, you depend on your team and they need your interpersonal skills; it is your job to defend them. Openness to discuss one's position and a positive attitude to a more engaged view often helps to avoid tension, saving time and resistance in the long run. By allowing the involvement of others, opening communication channels and placing value on your team views, you create a team building action. Your aim is to defend your team, enable them to make decisions and encourage them to engage in a risk-free environment, knowing that you will step in to help should they hit a roadblock. You are to keep your team informed and by doing so demonstrate trust, because sharing information can relieve stress. I am sure you can imagine the emotional state you could get into if your manager says to you, "Can we have a word in my office?" It may well be something not closely related to your job, but automatically as a human being, you think of something negative. Another example is: you hear a noise in your back garden in the middle of the night. Your first thought is: 'Someone is in the shed.' That someone could be a cat!

As you lead others, the success and failure of any communication is the responsibility of the leader.

> *"We must all hang together or most assure we shall hang separately"*

So here are 7 Steps to defend others:

1. Allow your team to tell you exactly what they need.
2. Remain a team player: make it clear you are part of the larger team.
3. Advocate for your team. Protect your team at belt-tightening time.
4. Take a bullet for them. They will remember your action.
5. Don't give in. You may have to take it on the chin sometimes.
6. Keep your eyes open and do everything reasonable to maintain or exceed your team's profitability.
7. Remember that we all have weaknesses.

Leavers to Leaders: Leading Others

Empower

In the previous chapter, we explored how important it is to look at people that you lead as people, taking a complete view of the person. When you join the military, you are looked at as a whole. You are fed, sheltered and clothed. If you have a family, they are also looked after; it is a big community and the resources are there for you to tap into. In this final chapter of leading others, we will look at the last letter in P.R.I.D.E, the letter 'E' for empower. As a leader, your aim is to grow others and allow them to become the best of themselves. So, first we look at delegation and then supervising. How a leader supervises his team has an impact on the motivational level of others.

People want to be recognised for the work they do and they want to be empowered. I was a JNCO (Junior Non Commissioner Officer) when I was asked to be the regiment military liaison with the French maritime unit and facilitate an exchange and also build a stronger relationship between the two regiments. It was a huge responsibility for a JNCO; I would translate the official documents and write the official letters for the regiment. When we were in France, I would be driving my CO, conducting introduction meetings on his behalf and get invited to lunch and dinner with other senior French officers. Was this a privilege? Maybe, but it came with huge responsibilities. At the time as well, my French was so good, that I would confuse the hell out of the French. The reality was my CO trained me well: he sent me away to master my communication and written skills, and I had the support of my troop commander. He was then a young officer. To this day, I have huge respect and also find myself very comfortable amongst high-profile individuals.

Part of empowering others is finding out their needs. We have a lot of time to talk with our subordinates in the military, finding out their needs, what's important to them, what they want to accomplish, what their personal goals are. There is a system to give feedback and a grade to see how you are progressing to the next rank. As a leader, you need to realise there is no limit to the value someone can bring to your organisation, as long as there is no worry about who gets the credit. So as a leader, get into the habit of giving out awards and recognising the success of others. Mentoring and counselling are very important aspects to measure the progress of your team – even in the military, we have both in place. I have always been a great admirer of the British Army – Be the Best. This is such a motivational motto and I still wonder how many service personnel really think of what it means. I left my phase two training, running 1.5 miles in under 8 minutes, a time record for me but when you are in the midst of winners (which in my case was the paras) there is no other way. You have to gravitate to their standard. Hence why to this day, I always make sure I am in the midst of the best people, and I also make sure my team are influenced by them.

So use consistent development counselling, or a coach and

mentoring techniques, and develop an effective plan of action to sustain strength and minimise weaknesses. When you counsel your team, they will automatically be counselling their team as well. People will emulate your behaviour. As your team grows, create a programme to measure their success and allow them to assume greater responsibility to develop themselves both personally and professionally. Paul Bennett, who has been the executive director for both Henley & Southampton School of Business, during my interview says that he spends on average 50 to 60 percent of his time developing his team. Leaders serve and we will see how this attitude of serving develops the organisation in the next chapter.

So far, we have looked at engaging, empowering, counselling and mentoring your team. As a leader, the environment you place your team in is also very important. Creating an open line of communication so they can express their ideas and concerns is very important. Do they work in a team? Do they help each other or do they concentrate on their job description? This comes down to the climate you set. Climate changes, and I remember when my CO left and we had a new CO, it was a different climate. Not in a bad way, but it was not the same. Some would be saying the old CO was good, but the new CO is great, while others would be saying the opposite. Remember people will come and go and this may well change the climate of the organisation, but make sure to set the temperature.

"Climate can change, but set the temperature."

Morale is how people feel about themselves, their team and their leaders. High morale comes from good leaders, shared experience and common respect. High morale holds a team together: your team will perform when they feel they are part of something important and compelling.

As you head a team, most certainly you will have your year's goals, Q1 to Q4. Remember at the end of the day, it is people who deliver result. Your people come as a package with skills and experiences, physical and spiritual needs, and they have aspirations. Make sure you focus on those needs. I once remember a story of a bricklayer who was working and someone stopped to ask him, "What is happening here? He answered, "We are building a new building four storeys high for a corporate firm." The same question was asked to another bricklayer a few metres down. He responded, "Here Sir, you have a four-storey building which will be employing 400 people and managing the pensions and investments of some of the richest people on this planet, and I hope to see my daughter work here. I've spoken to the boss already." This guy is motivated. He sees the big picture: he has found the time to reach out to the boss and find out about the site, and coming from a builder this is a powerful statement. He has already bought into the vision and hopes to see his daughter working in this building. That is empowerment at its best. Show your people the big picture; show them the dream.

Here are 7 steps to empower others:

1. Show others how your goals are aligned with the organisation.
2. Prove your team's value to one another.
3. Cultivate a positive outlook with your team members.
4. Encourage them to suggest new ideas or concepts that can improve the workplace.
5. Make your team indispensable.
6. Celebrate the big and small wins.
7. Find ways to go around your team to do what's best for the team.

CHAPTER 7

Leavers to Leaders Leading Organisations S.E.R.V.E

Selfless Service

In this final chapter, we will study the traits and characteristics that you will need to lead your organisation using my S.E.R.V.E. approach as a model. S.E.R.V.E stands for selfless service, ethics, reinvent, vital and excellence. One of the values of the British Armed Forces is selfless commitment. I recall during the early days of my training that I learnt not only a new culture but also British military values. I remember asking myself, 'why is this so important?' Having grown up in Mauritius, I am familiar with British culture: Mauritius was a British colony between 1810 and 1968, which was almost 10 years before I was born. Not far from where I grew up, in the central part of the island, is a town called Vacoas. Today it is occupied by the Special Mobile Force, a unit representing the military. It is housed in one of the most attractive parts of the city, in an early colonial building that is still in use today by the Special Branch of the police. The compound also hosts the Commando and Close Protection Unit. I remember going there to see my two uncles who were both part of the VIPSU (Very Important Person Security Unit), a protection team around the Prime Minister. The 'selfless service' values instilled by the British military are still in force today. Whether you enlist in the British Armed Forces or The Mauritius Special Mobile Force, you are expected to carry out your duty at all levels in a selfless manner. The military in the UK and around the world has an approach to leadership, which is powerful and can be implemented in any organisation, large or small.

'Selfless service' should also apply to businesses, non-profits and government agencies, and all organisations where people are the leaders. Regrettably, when you listen to many of these organisations, you can hear their message very clearly; it is all about them. Unfortunately, this is perhaps the language that worked well for the baby boomer generation. My own generation and especially those younger than me – the pre-millennials and millennials – are not interested in a 'buy from me' attitude. These generations want to know how they are affecting the world in a positive way. Laurence Fink, CEO of Blackrock, made this comment in a television interview:

"To prosper over time, every company must not only deliver financial performance, but also show how it makes a positive contribution to society."

As we saw in the previous chapter, the quality of organisational leadership depends on the values and character of the leader. At the top of your organisation you set the rules for others to follow. In this age of automation and digital innovation, you need a team using a selfless approach in order to survive. Simply having a mission statement, values and a strapline will not last; longevity will come through embracing change and leading with a selfless attitude. We can serve each other better by encouraging generations to work together and see things through each other's eyes. If you want to motivate others to do business with your organisation, you need to find out what their reason, purpose or cause is. People are not going to trade with you just because you have a charity status. In the UK in May 2018, the media has been focusing on negative Oxfam operations around the world. This has generated a lot of attention from the British people. Many years ago, I heard someone say something that stuck with me: 'We must understand that everyone listens to the same radio station. The radio station is WII-FM and the capital letters stand for What's In It For Me?' We must add to this, 'how does it benefit others?' If you want people to work with you, this is the information you need to share: you need to change their thinking, their capacity, motivate your team, with your Boards, with your partners and your audience.

One of my main motivations in joining the military was my love of physical fitness. In the military, we have the assault course where you have 6ft and 12ft walls to climb over in order to complete the task. By the time you get to it, you are usually completely soaking wet, covered in mud and tired. This is a team effort, and will take a minimum of two to get across. With a team of 12 or more it takes some serious thinking; to reach across you need to grab each other, push one another and get to the other side as fast as possible. You would normally take the weakest person first and leave the strongest member until last.

In the world of business, we need to understand that leaders and subordinates, employers and employees, are on the same side and have the same objectives. If they 'grab each other's hands' and work together in a selfless manner, then we not only maximise the full potential of the leaders, but the full potential of the organisation and the people we serve. As a leader, you need to be motivated, not only when the chips are up, but even more so when the chips are down. I was once given one of the best pieces of business advice by a former American chairman. He said 'Samuel, if you are not thanking twenty people a day in your organisation, you are doing something wrong.' This was a revelation to me. By our British nature we say 'please' and 'thank you' all the time, and my wife and I are always praised on the good manners of our three daughters. But this wasn't what he was saying. He was referring to something deeper than 'please' and 'thank you'; he was referring to being grateful and having an attitude of selfless service because the future beyond 2020 will be all about serving human beings whether by automation or via direct communication.

So here are my 7 steps for a selfless attitude:

1. Be grateful to others; go beyond 'please' and 'thank you' with your team.
2. Remember the 6ft and 12ft wall; it is a team effort.
3. Implement selflessness at the top of your organisation.
4. Have 'away days' to implement those key values in your team.
5. To be selfless you need to become fearless about change.
6. Plan quarterly but commit daily; leading is not just once a quarter.
7. Understand why you lead and why others should follow.

Leavers to Leaders: Leading The Organisation

Ethics

It is no secret that ethics has become a hot topic, with a number of good books and articles written on the subject. This is not a backlash against the various corporate scandals we've seen over the last few years. Ethics may actually be the next big thing in the workplace and in business practice as we move into 2020. The millennials want to deal with a company that has good-quality products but also makes a positive impact in the world. In this chapter, I will explain some of the reasons why ethics are important and how leaders without them will be vulnerable.

There are as many definitions of 'ethics' as there are books and articles written on the subject, but it boils down to this: you need to decide what is right and have the courage to do it. Ethics are all about doing the right things and building trust and goodwill as a result. You trust your doctor to have good ethics; they will not make you sick just so they can collect more fees for making you well again. In the same way, because of your ethics, you would hand back the extra £20 the bank teller mistakenly gave to you. Ethics should be like blood flowing through a leader's body. The role that ethics plays in customer decision making is quite simple, especially in a modern, developed economy characterised by a multitude of products and services. Imagine there are several sellers who provide the same products, with the same quality and at the same price. Which seller would you choose? You will naturally go with the one for whom you have the most trust. This means you have heard about them and may even have bought from them before. Having good ethics is the foundation of trust; people will not trust your organisation or your leadership if you do not have good ethics. They need to trust that if something is not right, it will get sorted out. If ethics means having the commitment to do right and the courage to carry it out, then your company must become a kind of advocate for the customer. If you want your organisation to be known and recommended to friends and families, you have to create ethics from the inside out.

For an organisation, ethics means operating in a way that constantly looks out for the customer's interests, and understanding the customer's situation whether that is good or bad news for your organisation. Another way to think of ethics, either personally or professionally, is to imagine what you would do if no one was watching. What would you do if you and your team were in the boardroom discussing a business problem and a customer was listening in on a conference call? What would you say? What would your team be saying? How would they talk? Would they be asking themselves if the customer is really listening to this meeting? And finally, would the customer agree with the point you are discussing or not? This is an idea that I hope to implement at some point with my own customers. Reality TV is everywhere, even in airports and cruise terminals. So how would you behave if your friends and family were able to follow you on reality TV at work? Nothing is more important to the long-term success of your company and you as the leader than to have the trust and confidence of your clients.

I believe that the military, and especially the British Armed Forces, are very high on ethics. Every service personnel is trained to shoot, and when you are in a conflict zone when life is at stake and hostile fire is coming at you, you need to have your ethics as a priority. Hence the rule of engagement that says; when under attack, fire may be returned effectively and promptly to stop hostile fire.

Have you ever signed up for something online and it was really easy and efficient to do, but when it came time to end the service, the cancellation process was long? Perhaps it required a phone call, or even an email to customer service and in the process you find yourself being charged? This practice is very common with those 30 days free trials. How does it feel? Do you feel trapped and like you have just been robbed? I have had a similar experience with Facebook ads recently. Having set up a campaign and indicated a certain result, who would you contact if the campaign was not effective? Have you ever returned something to a seller or online company because you made a mistake? In many cases, the company will charge you as much as a 20% fee for restocking. In the reverse situation, the company would most likely send you a 'free' shipping label, but would they listen if you said you would charge them a fee for the trouble they caused you? Here is another example: you have a problem that has cost you a lot of time already and now you are told the reason your problem can't be solved is due to company policy. Why would the customer be interested in your policy when you are not respecting theirs?

21 "BEING SIGNED UP TO A SERVICE...WHICH IS EASY ONLINE, BUT WHEN IT COMES TO END OF TIME CANCELLATION THIS PROCESS CAN BE LONG AND SOMETIMES COSTLY!!"

A good example of a company that has established good ethics is John Lewis in the UK. Their ethics were established more than 70 years ago in a slogan coined by John Spedan Lewis, '*Never knowingly undersold*'. The staff are all known as partners and participate in the company's profits and they make sure they have the best price on the market. I had an amazing experience with John Lewis when buying our 50" plasma TV. It came with a free 5-year warranty, which we had to use when it broke a few weeks before the warranty was about to expire. Not only was the TV taken away for repairs, but we were also given a replacement in the meantime.

For an organisation, ethics means operating in a way that constantly looks out for the customer's interests and doing the right thing. Ethics are what keeps an organisation striving in the short and the long term.

Ethics are worthy of a whole book, and if you are looking for an easy read and the encouragement, I would recommend 'Ethicability' by Roger Steare.

Here are 7 steps you can take to lead your organisation with ethical values:

1. Take some time out with your team to really think about your ethics.
2. Set some rules by putting yourself in the customer's shoes.
3. Are these rules helping you to act with integrity?
4. What is a fair and reasonable decision?
5. Do you have the courage to do it?
6. How would you act if the customer was in the room?
7. How would you build trust and respect?

Leavers to Leaders:
Leading Organisation

Re-Invent

In 2014, when I founded TriExForces Group, I wanted to have a strapline that would resonate with me; something that would make me get out of bed in the morning. It would have to be a line that I could stand for regardless of how we performed and regardless of the industry. And it would have to resonate with the people in the organisation too. I already knew that TriExForces would not be a single brand. So, on September 14th of that year, TriForceChauffeurs was created to provide a transportation service for senior leaders. Since then, we have launched a number of other brands, but the one thing that unites them all is our strapline 'To Serve'. Every year, around fourteen thousand members of the British Armed Forces transition from the military. For most, they embark onto their military journey as teenagers, and then disembark into a totally different world as an adult.

I am a strong believer that the military is a great stepping stone in life, and that if each of those transitioning out of the army used the principles outlined in the 7 steps, I have no doubt that they would make successful transitions into and even lead their chosen industry. Why? How can I be so confident? It all comes down to the 'Serve' principle. Those brave men and women have one thing that has kept them for either seventeen or twenty-two years in the Armed Services. Perhaps in the beginning it was about Queen and country, but then in times of pressure, it comes down to selfless service. The military around the world have handled change well in the past, and continue to do so now. However, the way we conduct warfare is not the same as in the nineteenth and twentieth centuries; technology has made it simpler and easier, and therefore more powerful than ever before. However, the things that remain, as far as the British Armed Forces are concerned, are the values, teamwork and discipline that have helped them to anticipate change and to always seek to improve.

In their book 'The Spirit to Serve', J.W. Marriot Jr. and Kathi Ann Brown discuss how they built their hotel empire. The first Marriot was opened in 1957, which they built to 1,500 hotels in 1997, and 2,000 hotels by the year 2000. Today, Marriot has over 6,500 hotels in 127 countries and if you happen to visit any one of them, you will experience nothing less than their 'selfless service', and understand how the message of the book 'The Spirit to Serve' is still valid.

Change is constant. Indeed, its pace is accelerating. Change is inevitable; trying to avoid it is futile. As with Marriot hotels, a disciplined, cohesive organisation rides out the tough times and will come out even stronger than when it started. As a leader, you need to be able to manage change through your organisation, your workplace, and your business. As a strategic leader, you must guide your organisation through the three LOS if your change initiatives are to make a lasting impact. At the top of the organisation, you must demonstrate urgency by illustrating not only the benefits but also the necessity of change. Communicate this vision to the rest of your organisation and empower your subordinates at all levels so that everyone is working together behind the same idea. This is your true role as a leader: vision must start at the top.

As Winston S. Churchill stated: "This is not the end. It is not even the beginning of the end. But it is, perhaps, the end of the beginning."

Transformational style is a key factor of success. You need to challenge your team to rise above their immediate personal needs and self-interests. Re-invention involves the growth of both the professional and the personal for the good of the organisation. Your role as a leader at the top of the organisation is to imagine and innovate, to help your team develop and create needs, ideas, new models, new strategies with technologies and applications that will set your organisation apart. To be successful, you will need to demonstrate both personal and organisational competence. That is where the entrepreneur in you takes over. Being purely functional is not your place. By being vital, you make a connection between internal and external players of your organisation in order to expand the outcomes to partners and lead your industry.

We have seen the results when leaders react to change defensively and then fail. The latest in the UK are Toys R Us, Cineworld and the Pound shops. Unfortunately, this reminds me of Blockbuster stores which disappeared in a similar way.

From my experience, organisations are more adaptable when the values and foundations are clearly executed across all departments and all levels.

William Bridges, author of 'The Way of Transition' says that the first requirement of change is that people let go of the past, in particular their old workplace habits.

Organisational and personal change go hand in hand. A look back to an earlier chapter shows us how we have to manage ourselves, our health, well-being, relationships with others, and our spiritual life. We must treat ourselves well as human beings. Regarding the future of work, we must lead the change and not just react to it.

Harvard professor, Rosabeth Moss Kanter, author of 'The Change Masters' and 'The Challenge of Organizational Change' has views on change and organisations which have had great influence on corporate thinking in recent years. She has expressed her views directly to organisations, and in many journal articles and books. In an interview at Harvard, she makes her next major statement since 'Challenge of Organizational Change'. She predicts that businesses which are only locally focused and do not know how to build global partnerships and relationships will lose out. Business is in a phase of massive change — just restructuring is not sufficient. Walls are being torn down and bridges must be built.[20]

Global businesses such as Amazon, Uber, Airbnb and Just Eat

---

[20] https://www.sciencedirect.com/science/article/pii/0263237394900418

have developed cross-border ties but had a large impact on local businesses. This argument leans on many fields of analysis – sociological, historical and political, amongst others. For example, one of the major challenges facing business people today is the tension between the globalising power of business and the localising power of politics. There are many examples of successful companies which have paid greater attention to what used to be considered external forces, and they have consequently managed change better. When I look at the careers of CEOs and senior leaders in companies introducing new strategies and change processes, as well as at new management styles, all the time there is also the need for emotional support for managers to meet the pressures of stress and turmoil. This is highly disregarded in the workplace.

Relationships are a key asset in an organisation's global operations. Supplier-customer relations and partnerships are growing rapidly in power and importance. Cross-cultural factors should be outsourced very carefully as explanations of global competitive advantage: it has now become easier for businesses to break down borders.

Finally, businesses and organisations which have only a local focus and do not know how to build global partnerships and relationships will lose out. We are in a phase of massive change; just restructuring is not sufficient. From the young age of 19 as a young Freeport officer, I became very curious about the business of importing and exporting. This led myself and my best friend, Yannick, to travel to Hong Kong and China for a few weeks to visit plants and manufacturing companies. Walls were being torn down and bridges had to be built.

22. AS A YOUNG BOY I WAS VERY CURIOUS ABOUT THE BUSINESS IN IMPORT & EXPORT

Here is a 7 steps action plan for you to lead change in the workplace:

1. Engage at all levels for imagination and innovation of new ideas, models and strategies.
2. Demonstrate personal and organisational competence supported by workplace training and development.
3. Connect internally and externally with partners who can expand the organisation.
4. Look at the mission, values, and organisation beliefs.
5. Appreciate the worth and input of your subordinates.
6. Examine who is leading change.
7. Let go of the past, and reinvent your team mentality.

Leavers to Leaders: Leading The Organisation

Being Vital

In Chapter 4, we briefly touched on being more vital and less functional, and we used the holiday scenario where in one example you have people really feeling your absence at work and in the other example they simply get on with things. A vital person is someone who is interdependent and actually connects the dots. A functional person is more independent and would rather work in his own space following his own agenda rather than working in a team environment. Both styles can be very effective in the workplace, but separating yourself from your team reduces your ability to understand their needs and foster their individual and team collaboration. Independent leadership gives a sense of supervision, speed and competency. But of course, the more you need to supervise, the more you need to manage. Micromanaging wastes your energy, undervalues your time and would annoy you and your team, which can lead to an unhealthy workplace atmosphere and affect staff turnover.

Someone who is interdependent is more vital. Other people like you so much that they miss you, and they like your work so much that they almost cannot function without you. In the military, we have special units. For example, in the US their special forces are the SEALs, the equivalent of our SAS and SBS. These are small teams who operate together or separately.

They spend enough time together that they can recognise the shadow of each member. They know his reactions, his feelings and emotions. They keep themselves on top form in order to maintain high team effort. Each and every one of them knows what they are good at, reliable for and they train very hard. Hence why they are the best. The SAS motto is 'Who Dares Wins' and those of the SEALs are: 'The Only Easy Day Was Yesterday', and 'It Pays to be a Winner'. Right from the outset, you have a clear picture of what to expect and what is expected of you. Only the best stay in the team, and their skills need to be up to date, otherwise they are a liability rather than an asset.

Daniel Priestley, author of 'Key Person of Influence' and co-founder of Dent Global, an organisation specialising in the development of entrepreneurs, describes this in his book:

"Functional people might be great at what they do, they might talk the talk and walk the walk, but the harsh reality is they are performing a role that is replaceable. If someone can find a cheaper option (automation) they will take it, because a functional person is just one possible solution to a problem. A company can down-size functional people. Functional does the job but functional is still interchangeable. People who are in functional jobs see themselves as competent when executing a set of processes. They try to get better at those processes and they make marginal improvements. Functional people try to stay up to date with the standards and they make sure they are able to perform as directed, but they secretly resist change and don't like new disruptive ideas."

Daniel also went on to explain what makes a vital person: "People who are performing a vital role see themselves as aligned to the result rather than the process. They ask questions about, 'why do we do things this way?' and 'what will it be like in the future?' Vital people are not worried about creating value. They want to deliver more of it, regardless of how it happens. No matter what, they will always adapt and change dynamically if it gets them more quickly towards a better result. A vital person knows that while they are gone, people are worried that they won't come back.

So being a vital person is like being a SEAL, an SAS in your work place. It is not good enough being just a member of a regiment; you need to be valuable and irreplaceable, bringing the highest results and focusing on the highest achievements. In a broad sense, a vital person is ready to disrupt the way things are done; they are constantly challenging the status quo and looking around to see if they can improve the things that they are doing. Most importantly, when they do spot something that needs to be changed, they do something about it. A vital person is a leader who lifts people up. In Chapter 4 we talked about livening up each other. As a leader, your role is to build morale, make people feel good about themselves, their team and their leaders. As we will see in the next chapter, high morale comes from good leadership, common values and mutual respect. As a leader, you should always be behind your team, setting the example, and inspiring them to pull together to achieve their objective. That's one of the most powerful ways to create morale. You should always plant the winning spirit in your people. You must have a commitment to do your best, no matter when, no matter what. A leader does not sit on the fence waiting to see which way the wind is blowing. As a leader, you need to communicate clearly about issues that could be affecting your workplace. The success and failure of any communication is the responsibility of the leader. And sometimes it pays to pause before your response.

As a vital leader, you need to develop the skill of listening; we have two ears and one mouth for a reason. In my LOS podcast, one chairman by emeritus of the third largest cruise line said: "Your last 20 years following your leadership years is all about listening to others. You listen to board members, staff and make your decision."

From a very young age, I have been interested in helicopters. I remember looking at the pictures of my uncle doing his Commando training and hanging onto those Lynx helicopters. When I was in the British military I had the thrilling pleasure to be at the back of a Chinook helicopter. We deployed many of them during Operation Telic and I was in charge of getting them loaded onto the ships. It was a dream job at the time. Just recently, I was on board the USS Harry S. Truman and, although it has some interesting fighter jets, I am always more interested with the Black Hawk helicopters.

So, today as an entrepreneur I am still interested in those flying machines, and I have come to discover that the best way to lead an organisation is to have a helicopter approach. Helicopters are versatile and can hover up and down, but do not have the resilience for long distance because they need refuelling. Leading an organisation requires you to hover down in order to get a better feel of the ground, but also when you are up, you get the best long view of the horizon to see where you are going. Even though fighter jets can also hover up and down, nowadays they certainly cannot land anywhere – unlike a helicopter. My clients and partners are able to witness this style of leadership in me.

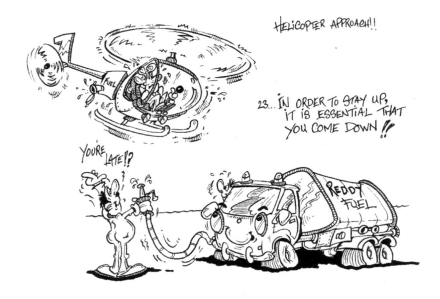

One of the most important duties of leaders is to develop their subordinates. Mentoring plays a vital part in developing competent and confident leaders. We don't know which of our subordinates today will become vital contributors and leaders in the future. Therefore, we need to strive to pass on our knowledge and skills to future leaders so that they can become their very best.

In the end, leaders leave a footprint and sometimes are best missed when they are away. I remember back in 1999, when my father passed away, we had over 1,000 people coming to pay their respects. It was then that I realised that he was a true leader. People would come from all backgrounds and walks of life, from his workplace and from the community he served as a police officer and also a pastor of the church. He was an accomplished leader. So, start with the end in mind: would your workplace and colleagues miss you if you were to leave your job? What would they say about you? (And I am not talking about gossiping or back-stabbing.)

Here are your 7 steps to becoming a vital leader:

1. Be results-orientated.
2. Get ready to challenge the status quo.
3. Ask why, and be ready to offer an alternative for your why.
4. Produce more.
5. Use the helicopter analogy; hover down to get a better view of the ground and up to get a long-distance view.
6. Be a torch and light the way and guide others.
7. Watch out for those that are functional; they may be your biggest challenge, so learn to lead them.

Leavers To Leaders: Leading Organisation

Excellence

In previous chapters, we have looked at selfless service, the importance of ethics, re-inventing the company, the role of being vital and values in the workplace. The last E in S.E.R.V.E. stands for excellence. How does a company create excellence? If you are in a large or small organisation, every minute of the day your company Is going up or down in value. I am not talking about your stock value, but the economic value as a business. Each time you and your company make a decision, every action you take, each time a customer has an interaction with your product or services, your company is either increasing or decreasing in value.

We often see shares going down based on a decision made by a company. If you run a small enterprise and don't handle a customer's complaint properly, this may have an impact on the actual value of the company, as they may not spend any more with you. Due to technological progress, it is now possible to measure those changes, and understand customers' behaviour and buying patterns. The future will only bring us more insight through technology. For example, depending on the product or service, the customer may spend up to 10 hours researching the market before finally making a decision to buy. The ZMOT (Zero Moment Of Truth) is a power report created by Google which is evidence of this new trend[21]. So, as a leader, regardless of your field, you need to understand the power of your customers.

24 You NEED TO THiNK ABOUT THE IMPACT OF YOUR ACTiONS, ON YOUR CUSTOMER, WITH ONLINE SOCiAL MEDiA, FRiENDS, FAMiLY, COLLEAGUES...CONNECTIONS ARE SO POWERFUL THESE CAN MAKE A DiFFERENCE ON THE OUTCOME!!

People around the world are talking, blogging, vlogging, texting, emailing, posting and networking more than ever before, making us all ever-more connected. This connection enables people to share opinions about you and your organisation much more easily, and those opinions have power. As a leader, you need to be aware of your actions and reactions at all times. Gone are the days where you could hide behind a screen or behind the telephone. As described in the last chapter, you must imagine that your customers – the people you serve – are in the room. The connection between people is so powerful that you

---

21 https://www.thinkwithgoogle.com/marketing-resources/micro-moments/zero-moment-truth/

now need to think not just about the impact of your actions on one customer, but also their friends, colleagues, family members and their online friends too.

Years ago, when I first arrived in London, I used to buy international calling cards which came in £5, £10, or £15 values. If you have friends and family scattered around the world, then perhaps you may remember them. Each £5 gave you a certain amount of time, normally in minutes, and in the last 15 seconds you had a horrible reminder that the call was about to finish. This forced you to get your priorities right when talking with friends and family. Now, I can pick up the phone and ring my mother at any time, and sometimes if she is too slow at picking up, I am already on a different social platform. It is that easy to communicate globally. In 2010, the world population was 6.8 billion, and 26% were online. By 2020, 66% of the 7.6 billion population will be online – an increase of 3 billion[22]. The pace of change is accelerating daily, and if you are not improving your products and services, tomorrow they will be just a commodity. So, not only do you need to be constantly changing, but also combining the creative power of your subordinates and your customers. You have to create a climate of excellence and improve on complaints, other people's differences, and agree that you always need to be improving. Increasingly, you need a culture of excellence in your organisation and to use the Leader's Operating System – the 3 LOS – to keep you ahead of the pack. Each of the 3 LOS has been a preparation for you in

---

[22] https://www.internetworldstats.com/stats.htm

Leading Oneself, Leading Others and finally Leading the Organisation. My aim, however, is to help you recognise that these ideas are interconnected and then to weave them together, allowing you to re-invent yourself and your organisation model or your business. As I have outlined, a culture of excellence breeds a much more fundamental shift than you realise.

People don't work day to day in the "big picture". They work in the smaller details, tasks of your organisation and its business. Not that the big picture is irrelevant, but it is the little things that make a big impression, that send a message of excellence.

Back in 2001, my first job was at the Mauritius Freeport Authority. Gerard Sanspeur, the CEO, decided to implement Kaizen, meaning "good change" – a Japanese theory, based on the belief that continuous, incremental improvement adds up to substantial change over time across all sections of the organisation. I remember this very well, because it shifted the way we thought of our customers and how we did every single task. Kaizen would document every detail, even the way a pallet is moved from A to B and how to improve this activity. The decision to have this rolled out across all departments was a corporate decision and it worked. Going into 2020, these types of standards would need to be more visible to the customers rather than just being an internal standard. And if it is not increasing the excellence in service to the customer, then they will most likely it find it useless. Now that you are in the spotlight, you can succeed or fail a lot faster. An example of some of those companies that have been in the spotlight that come to mind are Walmart vs Amazon, Vodafone vs WhatsApp, Hilton vs Airbnb, Avis vs Uber, and Sky vs Netflix. These companies are all competing in the same industry differently using digital innovation. A culture of excellence will allow your company to become more resilient, creative, innovative and adaptive to the technology shift.

Henry Ford, founder of the Ford Motor Company, famously said:

"Whether you think you can, or think you can't – you're right."

As a leader, your role is to create a growth mindset for excellence, and sometimes you need to communicate in a way that will promote this mindset.

For example:

"Great job, now let's see how we can improve on that for the next time."

"That didn't work. Let's talk about how you approached it and what might work better."

"This is hard. Don't feel bad if you can't do it yet."

Here are 7 action tips to help you maintain a culture of excellence:

1. Create more value at all times.
2. Engage with your team but get the customer involved too.
3. Empower your team with a growth mindset from the start.
4. Use a good coaching programme that engages your team in fun, creative way.
5. Understand what makes your team tick, and act upon that. Foster positive working environments across the generations.
6. Consider a 'helicopter approach'; hover up and down to take a close-up and long-term view of your organisation.
7. Remember to treat people as individuals and not as one, as this will enable you to recruit people who are "made for the job" as opposed to those that are "able to do the job".

Leavers to Leaders Epilogue:

A Unique Opportunity

When I was 15, my first job during the school holidays was as a builder. You may wonder why I chose to be a builder, which is such hard work. The day is long, from 8:00am until 5:00pm, shovelling sand, brick, cement and rock-sand to make concrete. I enjoyed the physical work and it meant that I didn't have to go to the gym. It was no surprise when, with my first monthly pay cheque, I bought myself a set of weights, two dumbbells and one barbell. Pretty soon, I was fit and had a well-toned body and a six pack; a good advantage at that age, Especially when I had to take my top off on a hot day at the beach in Mauritius. When I decided to reinvent myself in London in 2001, I knew it would be quite hard to settle and may be impossible to attend a gym, so I took my two dumbbells with me. My luggage was 75kgs, and I have no idea how those baggage handlers felt when they tried to move it. Luckily, though, my girlfriend at the time (now my wife) was a ground operator for the airline, and I was also well known at the airport as a Freeport officer. Did I use those weights in England? You bet I did. Finsbury Park in North London was my new training ground, especially after I got accepted into the British Armed Forces. I trained hard with running too, and got my mile and a half down to eight minutes.

I've done my best to demonstrate the Leader's Operating System that underpins truly outstanding leadership. I've given you an immense amount of detail and evidence, and I expect few of you will remember every little detail in this book.

We are living in the greatest time for humanity because, for the very first time, we have four generations in the workplace at the same time. In the US, almost 40% of workers have a leader that is younger than they are, and that number is growing rapidly. The power is shifting like never before because of our increased reliance on digital intelligence. We see young people starting in their early twenties and scaling up to global presence by the time they reach their thirties. Baby boomers are healthier and more vibrant, with longer lives. For many of them, it is a harsh reality when they suddenly lose their job and the phone stops ringing. Is it possible that, in a digital world, we see experience as a liability rather than an asset? Or, when it comes to the power in the workplace, today's thirties are the new fifties? Being relevant – the ability to use timeless wisdom and apply it to modern-day problems – is important. It is time to stop casting judgement on the young and instead use curiosity to match your wise eyes with their fresh eyes. To be a leader in your field, you must be enthusiastic about life, deal with other people graciously, and encourage them to lead the organisation. When you behave in a more friendly and outgoing manner, it can be enormously helpful to you socially, professionally and even spiritually. Being in transition could be the best thing to happen to you, whether you've completed a full service in the military or just had enough of your current job. Take a look at the mountain of values you are already standing on. This is your opportunity; there couldn't be a better time to reinvent yourself. If you are coming out of the military, it is likely that you are going through a resettlement, and this is the best time to use this opportunity. I have interviewed over 25 people about the LOS concept, and will continue to do so in the years to come as I focus on the 3 LOS of Leadership.

As a reminder here are the 7 lessons that we learnt from each LOS:

Leading opportunity:

1. Be sincere in yourself and show appreciation when leading opportunities.
2. Remember 'Opportunity Is No Where' can also be seen as 'Opportunity Is Now Here'.
3. Don't criticise, condemn, or complain.

Liven up others:

1. Be genuine and passionate about people.
2. Be your best.
3. Re-energise others; no one wants to listen to another complainer.

Listen to others:

1. Listen to understand rather than to respond.
2. Use other people's brains.
3. Make your case bigger than your ego.
4. Network effectively for collaboration.

Learn from others:

1. Ask for help.
2. You don't have to be the cleverest person In the room.
3. Adopt a learning attitude.
4. Try to learn from others' mistakes.
5. Find time to refocus.

Leading oneself:

1. You are the most important person.
2. Use the 7 tips to stay healthy.
3. Manage your social being.
4. Work on your spiritual being.
5. Understand your emotional needs.
6. Become more used to engaging with multi-generations.

Leading others:

1. Promote your staff and lead a diversity culture.
2. Train others to lead.
3. Defend the well-being of your team.
4. Empower them to succeed.

Leading the organisation:

1. Selfless service is about ensuring that people and organisation are of equal importance.
2. Change is everywhere; you need to continuously re-invent your business.
3. The two V's = Being Vital and Value.

4. Foster a spirit of excellence.
5. Become environmentally friendly.

As I write 'Leavers to Leaders', I hope to share information and inspiration which will make a difference in your life. My hope is that some of the Leader's Operating System (LOS) has struck a chord with you, and that this will help you lead a more enjoyable and effective life in future. I hope and believe that the principles taught in 'Leavers to Leaders' will help you reap those rewards and become the leader you ought to be.

If you look around your company right now, you can probably put your finger on at least a dozen specific items which are not in line with its core ideology, or that impede progress. Somehow, inappropriate practices have crept in. Attaining alignment in oneself, others and the organisation is not just a process of adding new things; it is also a never-ending process of identifying and correcting misalignments that push a leader away from their core ideology. If a position prevents your progress, change your role or move. If the company strategy and ideology is misaligned with your own, bring change to the company.

At the heart of the LOS, we have three important frameworks, and a clear and expressive description of what you must do to lead yourself, others and the organisation. This framework is adapted to fit the work of leaders from the military, private, non-profit, SMEs and public organisations to show you the three legs you should be standing on as a leader. I have learnt so much myself by writing this book, and as you may have noticed,

I am also in a transition. Maybe this book should have been called 'Leaders in Transition'! I will be doing some intense travelling to preach the LOS and help many to take the leap in coming years. But as you walk away from reading this book, I hope you will take away three key concepts to guide your thinking for the duration of your career and pass on to others. These concepts are:

1. Be comfortable being uncomfortable.
2. Be the architect of your own life.
3. Seek alignment within yourself first; take care of number one.

So, this is not the end. Nor even the beginning of the end. But it is, I hope, the end of a beginning where you decide to re-invent yourself and take on new challenges to be the very best leader. Write to me with your stories and feedback and connect with me @SamuelTReddy on Facebook, LinkedIn and Twitter, or you can write to my office at: info@TriExForces.com. Finally, if you are wondering if I am a writer then the answer is no. Deep inside me, I know I have a message that can help people. I certainly knew I would be an entrepreneur at a young age of nine, but never imagined I would be a writer. I look forward hearing from you.

Yours,
Samuel
www.SamuelTReddy.com